In
The
Middle

by Barry Oshry

4/03

ISBN 0-910411-15-8

Table Of Contents

Still Circling After All These Years

It has been said of certain performing artists — chief among them Leonard Cohen, poet and songwriter — that "they are not moving forward, they are circling round and back, reconnoitering the original occasion… trying finally to get the ancient thing right."[1] Anyone familiar with my work over the past twenty years could say the same of me — I do not move ahead, I circle round and back, scratching at the same old territory, hoping with each cycle to unearth a shiny nugget or two.

I have been fascinated with middle dynamics ever since our first Power & Systems Laboratory in 1972 when we created an experimental learning community of Elites (Tops), Immigrants (Bottoms), and Managers (Middles). Of the three classes, the Middles were the least dramatic — the real action was above them or below them, or so it seemed. The Middles were a hard-working lot, focused on doing a competent job, humorless, honest, playing it straight, committed to saving the system from self-destruction, and, for the most part, finding precious little acknowledgement — if not downright abuse — for their efforts.

Over the years I have watched group after group step into that middle space, and year after year similar patterns emerge as Middles struggle to survive and function in a space in which they are torn between the needs, demands, pressures, and priorities of those above them and those below them, and in which they are pulled apart from one another and thereby deprived of the comfort and support of their peers.

Some say that life in the middle is not easy, but there are several things which are all too easy in the middle: it's easy to be alone, to feel unsupported, to be seen as ineffective by both those above and those below; it's easy to become the scapegoat for system failures; it's easy to feel weak, confused and incompetent; and it's easy to take all of this personally.

But of course, none of this can be personal. We find the same middle pattern wherever we go — supervisors and department heads, chairpersons and middle managers; we find the pattern in manufacturing and high tech, in health care and

---

[1] Leon Wieseltier, *"The Prince of Bummers,"* **The New Yorker**, July 26, 1993.

universities, in the military and religious institutions; wherever there are middle positions there is every likelihood of finding the familiar middle pattern.

Over the years I've circled around the following questions: What is the nature of this middle space? How does it affect individuals, and how does it affect middle groups? And what is the possibility of empowerment in the middle space, individually and collectively?

Although there is a certain sameness to "organization" wherever you find it — familiar patterns occurring again and again — there are also the rare "mutations," the out-of-the-ordinary variations. Some "mutations" are failures, even less effective than the usual disempowering patterns. But every so often a "mutation" occurs which produces a remarkably different and positive result. And it is the rare mutation which points the way to new and productive possibilities in the middle.

The following chapters were written over a thirteen year period, from 1980 to 1992. Each chapter scratches at, and ultimately illuminates, another piece of the middle puzzle. Chapter I focuses on the individual in the middle; Chapter II deals with the Middle Group; and Chapter III presents a comprehensive framework for mastering the middle space. In each section, we present both the usual disempowering pattern of middle life and the "mutation" which points the way to new, more empowering possibilities.

This investigation of middleness began in our educational simulations of organizations and societies. Our findings intrigued practitioners — both consultants and managers — who found that our results in the laboratory closely mirrored their experiences in the field. Some were stimulated to undertake new approaches to middle empowerment. Some of these are described in Chapter III. The investigation — in both the laboratory and the field — is ongoing. The results are promising. This book is intended to illuminate middle dynamics, but it is also an invitation to you to join that ongoing investigation.

Barry Oshry
January 1, 1994
Boston, Massachusetts

Chapter 1

MIDDLE POWER —

Person in the middle

Middleness

Middleness is not a *position*; it is a *condition*. It is a condition all of us experience, at various times and in varying degrees, in whatever position we are in, whether we are at or near the top, on the bottom, or in the middle of the organization hierarchy.

Middleness is the condition in which we exist between two or more individuals or groups; these groups have differing priorities, perspectives, goals, needs and wants; and each of them exerts pressure on us to function on its behalf.

Middleness is a potentially dis-empowering condition. It tends to weaken *individuals* in the middle: confusing them, muddling their strategies, sapping their energies; and it tends to weaken *groups* in the middle: alienating members from one another, and diminishing their capacity to function as an integrated and effective unit.

Middleness is also a potentially empowering system condition. It offers individuals and groups unique opportunities for sensitive and effective influence over the course of system life.

Which way it goes for us when we are in the middleness condition — toward powerlessness or power — depends on our ability to understand and manage the unique dynamics of that condition.

In a previous paper[1] we analyzed the dynamics of the middle group; in this our focus is on the individual in the middle.

---

[1] See Chapter 2 and *"Middle Group Dynamics: Ramifications for the OD Unit"* in **Trends and Issues in OD Current Theory and Practice.** W. Warner Burke and Leonard D. Goodstein (eds.), University Associates, Dan Diego, CA, 1980.

Middleness In New Hope And Micro-System

The analysis in this paper is based heavily on our experiences over the past several years with NEW HOPE and MICRO-SYSTEM, two learning environments designed to sharpen and clarify the following common system conditions:

TOPNESS: that condition in which we have overall responsibility for a system or piece of a system, in which we are the creators or custodians of the system's rules and institutions, and in which we control the distribution of resources others value.

BOTTOMNESS: that condition in which we feel constrained by system rules, institutions and structures made by others, and in which we have no control over the distribution of resources we need or want.

MIDDLENESS: that condition in which we are caught up between the worlds of others, pushed and pulled and torn by their perspectives, priorities, and demands.

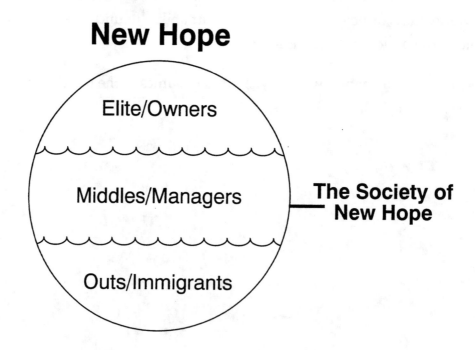

New Hope

Elite/Owners

Middles/Managers — **The Society of New Hope**

Outs/Immigrants

The Society of New Hope is the experiential component of the Power & Systems Laboratory.[2] In New Hope a three-class social system is created comprised of the Elite/Owners, the Middles/Managers, and the Outs/Immigrants. New Hope is a total immersion experience which lasts anywhere from 24 hours to five days and which involves many elements of people's lives during that period: how much personal property they have, where and how well they live and eat, the work opportunities available to them, the amount of money they have and are able to earn, their roles and responsibilities in the society, and so forth.

Topness is the predominant element of the Elite position. The Elite own and control all of the property and territory of New Hope: its buildings, sleeping accommodations, food and dining facilities, currency, materials, and supplies. The Elite control the availability of work in the society; they determine the wages to be paid for labor and they set the prices for goods. The Elite control the society's legislative and judicial processes. And the Elite can use their control over resources and structure any way they choose. They are accountable to no one.

Bottomness is the predominant element of the Out/Immigrant position. Outs enter the society with little more than the clothes on their backs. They have few personal belongings, no money, no property, nor do they have any rights to property. There are laws in New Hope, but adherence to these laws is more in the interest of the Elite than the Outs. (There is, for example, a law protecting private property, but the Elite are the only ones who own property; there is a law prohibiting actions aimed at overthrowing the existing order which is essentially a social order favoring the Elite; there is a legislative process whereby the laws of New Hope can be changed, but the Chief Justice of New Hope, a member of the Elite, has veto power over all legislation.) The Outs exist in a system in which they have minimal access to those resources they need or want, minimal control over the distribution of those resources, and minimal control over the rules, structures, and institutions that influence their lives.

Middleness is the predominant element of the Middle/Manager position. Middles occupy the professional and managerial positions in New Hope. They have no direct control over the distribution of New Hope resources, nor over the laws, structures, and institutions of the society. Middles are responsible for

[2] For further information see *"Power and The Power Lab"* by B. Oshry in **New Technologies in Organization Development**, W. Warner Burke (ed.) University Associates, La Jolla, CA, 1975; and "Prospectus for the Power & Systems Laboratory," Power & Systems, Inc., Boston 1980.

managing, on behalf of the Elite, the institutions and work of New Hope. Given their position between Elite and Outs, and given the marked discrepancies between Elite and Outs in access to and control over valued resources, Middles find themselves caught between two parts of the system with very different interests, perspectives, needs, and desires.

Micro-System

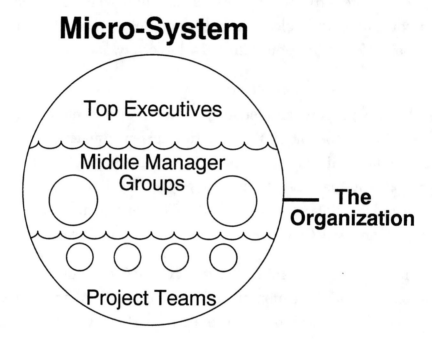

Micro-System is a shorter term system experience (2 to 3½ hours in duration) in which, as in New Hope, a social system is created with topness, bottomness, and middleness conditions. There is a Top Executive group with total control over the organization's budget and structure; there are Project Team Members who do the direct work of the organization and who have no control over its structure or the distribution of its resources; and there are the Middle Managers with both staff and line functions who manage the work of the system and mediate the interactions between Top Executives and Project Team Members.

New Hope and Micro-System isolate and sharpen the conditions of topness, middleness, and bottomness. These conditions exist more clearly and more purely in these laboratory settings than they do in most other organizational settings where any given position is likely to be a less tidy mesh of relationships with shifting and overlapping components of topness, middleness, and bottomness. In

New Hope and Micro-System we attempt to approximate a purity of experience which rarely exists in the natural world. We do so, recognizing the limitations of this approach, in order to isolate and clarify the characteristics of each element of the whole.[3]

Our focus here is on middleness. The questions we will address are these: How does the middleness condition influence the experiences of individuals existing within that condition? What are the unique stresses and strains associated with the middleness condition? What are the characteristic responses people make in their efforts to cope with these stresses and strains? What is the special power of middleness? What factors need to be dealt with in order for that power to be realized? And what are the payoffs and costs to the individual that come with increased middle power?

[3] This procedure is similar to that employed by the nuclear physicist who maintains, for example, that the photon, the unit of light, is merely an abstraction created by the conditions of the laboratory experiment itself, that there are no pure photons in the physical world, and that the physical world "is an unbroken pattern of wholeness that presents itself to us as webs… of relations." Gary Zukov in **The Dancing Wu Li Masters: An Overview of the New Physics**, Morrow, New York, 1979.

The Middle Person

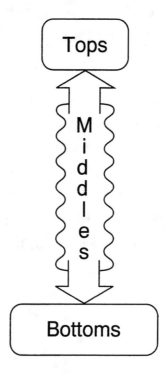

New Hope and Micro-System sharpen the personal dilemmas of middleness: What is it like for us to be caught between two or more individuals or groups in conflict with one another? In New Hope and Micro-System Tops and Bottoms are at odds over any number of fundamental issues: whether the system itself is legitimate or illegitimate; whether its rules, structures and procedures should be maintained or changed; whether change — if there is to be any — should be gradual or dramatic; what is to be an equitable distribution of system resources and who should decide that; how particular crisis situations should be handled; and so on. In the midst of these issues are the Middles, on the one hand responsible for managing the work of the system, and on the other caught up in an endless series of disputes between Tops and Bottoms. They are pushed and pulled and subjected to a variety of pressures. Tops and Bottoms may attempt to enlist their support and assure their loyalty on any number of issues; Tops and Bottoms may try to use Middles as extensions of themselves — as spokespersons, messengers, mediators; they may try to use Middles to buffer themselves against intrusions or confrontations; they may try to win Middles over to their positions through rational debate or by menacing them, cajoling them, co-opting them, or drawing on their sympathies. This then is the condition of middleness, focused and sharpened.

Observations From New Hope and Micro-System.

There is in New Hope and Micro-System a common pattern of middleness which has the following elements:

1. Middles tend to be involved in a hectic work pace. Middles generally work long and hard throughout the duration of these system experiences. They are continually on the go, doing their management work, meeting with Tops and with Bottoms, bearing messages, structuring and restructuring the work, mediating, negotiating, and so forth. It is an illuminating experience (and often an aerobic one) to track the life of a Middle in New Hope for a thirty-minute period. In contrast to the relatively stationary existences of Tops and Bottoms, Middles tend to be in perpetual motion. They carry in their heads a seemingly endless list of items to be accomplished: quick management meetings with Tops, setting up work for Bottoms, back to Tops on some other matter, an errand to run, paper work to be cleaned up, a piece of business to be transacted on the run between one meeting and another, and on and on it goes.

2. The middle experience tends to be an ego-deflating one. As hard as Middles work, they generally receive very little positive support, reinforcement or gratitude from either Tops or Bottoms. Middles tend to feel that they are not measuring up to the standards both Tops and Bottoms hold for them. Words Tops and Bottoms have used to describe them include: confused, uncertain, wishy-washy, unable or unwilling to take a stand, spineless, powerless, weak. On the other hand, Middles are also described as hard working, well meaning, and trying to please. According to Tops and Bottoms, the problem with Middles lies less with their intentions and effort than with their competence.

3. The middle experience tends to be a confusing one. Middles tend not to have clear and firm positions on issues. Their thinking is often muddled. They listen to Tops and the Tops' position makes sense to them; they listen to Bottoms and their position also makes sense. Middles find themselves confused and ambivalent on a variety of issues, unable to make up their minds, continually

flip-flopping between contradictory positions, or, in attempting to be responsive to both Tops and Bottoms, assuming compromise positions which satisfy neither.

4. Middles tend to believe that the significant action in the system lies with the Tops and the Bottoms and not with themselves. Middles have described themselves as "telephone wires" connecting the Tops and the Bottoms, as "invisible people" through whom the feelings and actions of Tops and Bottoms flow. Despite these feelings of insignificance, Middles generally feel a heavy responsibility for keeping the system together, for making it work, for preventing Tops and Bottoms from destroying one another and the system.

5. Middles tend to feel isolated and lonely in the system. They are accepted by neither Tops nor Bottoms, and their own groups tend to be fractionated.[4] Middle group members tend to be non-supportive of one another and there is often a good deal of interpersonal tension and competition among them.

6. Middles tend not to take independent action. Tops and Bottoms are more likely to develop game plans and strategies and to initiate actions based on these. Middles, by contrast, tend to be more reactive, acting in support of or against the plans of others, or reconciling the conflicting game plans of Tops and Bottoms. Middles rarely develop a middle perspective of their own, one which is independent of the perspectives of Tops and Bottoms.

7. Middles tend to personalize their experiences, attributing whatever difficulties they are having to their own personal failings in skill, character or intelligence. Better persons, they believe, would be less confused, less ambivalent, less wishy-washy. Better persons would be able to handle their situation more competently, more powerfully.

---

[4] See Chapter 2 and B. Oshry, **Middle Group Dynamics: Ramifications for the OD Unit.**

Middleness As A Personally Dis-Integrating Space

Middleness is a diffusing space. It pulls people outward.

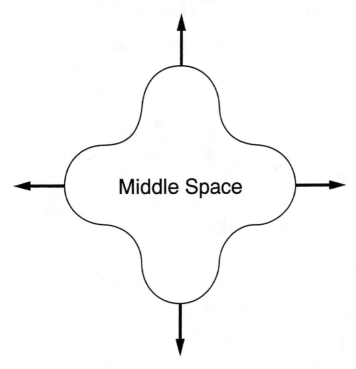

A group positioned in a middle space tends to diffuse through the system.

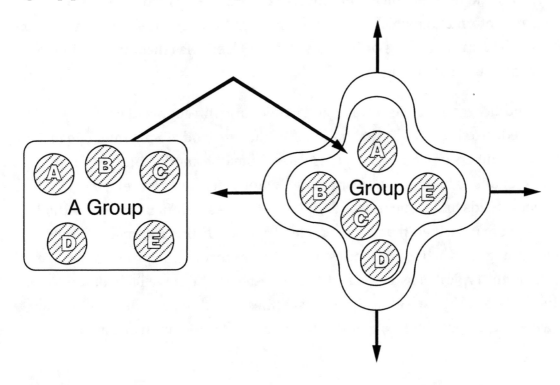

An individual positioned in a middle space tends to diffuse through the system.

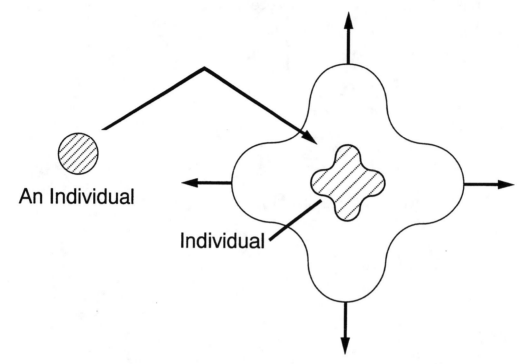

An Individual

Individual

Diffusion is the source of the unique power of the Middle. Diffusion provides contact with and information about different parts of the system, and it is that contact and information which makes it *possible* for Middles to see the total system more clearly than either Tops or Bottoms and which enables them to function in a sensitive and informed manner.

But middleness, when its diffusing dynamics are unrecognized and unmanaged, also leads to dis-integration. Middleness tends to dis-integrate groups such that members grow increasingly isolated from one another and the group becomes unable to function as an integrated whole, (see next figure) and middleness tends to dis-integrate individuals. It makes it difficult for individual Middles to organize their many, varied, and often conflicting internal thoughts, beliefs, feelings and action tendencies into coherent forms. The problem for Middles in the typical New Hope and Micro-System pattern we have described is not the absence of ideas, feelings and possibilities for action; it is that Middles are overwhelmed by possibilities, many of which are in conflict with one another.

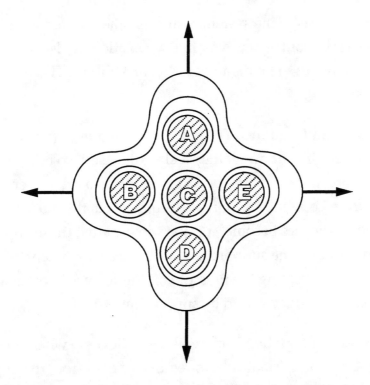

In the dis-integrated middle group, members become increasingly isolated and out of touch with one another; they function independently of one another and often in conflict with one another; and the group as a whole is unable to function in an integrated manner.

Middles interact with Tops and from those interactions particular patterns of thought, feeling, and action possibilities emerge. Middles interact with Bottoms and from those interactions other patterns of thought, feeling, and action possibilities emerge. Many of these patterns are in direct conflict with one another. As a result, Middles see the demands of Tops as reasonable *and* as unreasonable, they feel empathy for Bottoms *and* antagonism toward them, they want to support Bottoms in their efforts to change the system *and* they want to subvert them, and so on. Given the diffusing experiences of Middles, all of these are possible ways for Middles to experience themselves, others, and the system as a whole. Rational and ethical cases can be made for all of these alternatives, even though various ones of them may be in direct contradiction.

When we are in topness or bottomness relationships we are less likely to experience these difficulties with internal integration. The more firmly entrenched we are on a given piece of the hill, the more likely we are to develop a coherent pattern of thought/feeling/action which is consonant with that position. Middles do not have that luxury; they see too much and know too much.

Contact with many parts of the system, which is inherent to the middle position, and which is the source of power in that position, is also a major contributing factor to the personal dis-integration of Middles. There are other contributing factors:

1. **Pressures from Tops and Bottoms.** The more dis-integrated Middles are, the more confused, uncertain, and weak they feel and are seen to be, the more likely Tops and Bottoms are to increase the pressure on them to bring them into line. As this pressure from Tops and/or Bottoms is increased, the more confused, uncertain and weak Middles become. It is paradoxical that those Tops and Bottoms who want to gain the support of Middles are more likely to succeed by *decreasing* rather than increasing the pressure on them, by acknowledging the special tensions of their position, and by supporting *them*.

2. **The hectic work pace.** Integration is more likely to develop when one is able to step back from the system periodically, to remove oneself from the ongoing pressures, to rest, to take a detached look at oneself, others, and the system as a whole. Getting out of the work flow from time to time is one element in this. Having a space of one's own to retreat to and conduct business in is another. But, the more Middles allow themselves to be carried along in the frantic flow of activities, being ever responsive to others, putting out fires, bearing messages, cleaning up the paper work, and so forth, the less opportunity there is for Middles to develop their own independent perspective on the system and to develop their own independent action strategies. Middles need to do the work of the system but in order to prevent personal dis-integration, they also need to pay special attention to their personal boundaries, to control their own involvement in the flow of work, to shut off periodically their responsiveness to others, to attend more often to themselves, to develop and protect their own personal space.

3. **Absence of support group.** Middleness is a potentially dis-integrating condition for groups as well as for individuals. When the dynamics of middleness go unrecognized and unmanaged, middle group members tend to drift apart, to become increasingly independent of one another, more isolated from one another, more interpersonally distant from one another, more competitive, less interested

in one another's work, less collaborative, and less personally supportive. It is this lack of peer group support which contributes to the personal dis-integration of Middles. Given the diffusing dynamics of middleness, Middles need to work much harder than Tops and Bottoms to develop an effective support system.[5] Minimally a strong middle team provides individual Middles with emotional support in trying situations. Beyond that it provides a setting for sharing and sorting through information about the system, for stepping back from the ongoing work and using these data to gain a larger perspective on system processes and issues, and for developing coherent middle strategies.

4. **Definition of the middle role.** The middle role is often defined by Middles as well as by Tops and Bottoms as one in which Middles are *expected* to be responsive to others. The role is positioned such that Middles believe they are supposed to be emissaries *of* others, extensions *of* others, negotiators *for* others, buffers *for* others. Such role definitions encourage Middles to see situations more from the perspectives of others and less from their own perspective. Such definitions encourage Middles to act in the interests of specific others rather than in the interests of the system as a whole. Middles need to recognize that middleness is more than a "telephone wire" between Tops and Bottoms, that it is its own legitimate position within the system, that there is a legitimate perspective that goes with middleness that is different from the perspectives of Tops and Bottoms, and that there is a legitimacy to independent actions in the middle, actions which may not be perceived by either Tops or Bottoms as particularly responsive but which in fact do serve the best interests of the system.

These are some of the factors which contribute to the personal dis-integration of Middles:

▲ the many and varied contacts Middles have throughout the system, each of which generates its own pattern of thoughts, feelings and action possibilities for Middles, and many of which are in conflict with one another;

▲ the tendency of Tops and Bottoms to respond to middle difficulties by increasing the pressure on Middles;

---

[5] See Chapter 2 and B. Oshry, **Middle Group Dynamics: Ramifications for the OD Unit.**

▲ the hectic work pace which when unmanaged makes it difficult for Middles to step back and gain some perspective on themselves and the system;

▲ the absence of a middle support group which itself tends to dis-integrate under the pressure of the middle condition; and

▲ the tendency to define middle positions as responsive and reactive rather than as independent and proactive.

All of these factors contribute to the personal dis-integration of Middles. This tendency toward dis-integration is the fundamental pitfall of middleness. It is highlighted under the time and structural pressures of New Hope and Micro-System, but it is a common theme for Middles in less dramatic situations as well. The confusion, uncertainty, wishy-washiness, incompetence, and non-groupness of middleness are not reflections of the personal characteristics of those people who are in the middle. The New Hope and Micro-System experiences repeatedly indicate that those are characteristic outcomes for whatever collection of people happen to be assigned by chance to middle positions. It is clear, then, that we are dealing not with system issues which are caused by personal failings but with personal difficulties which are the outcomes of unrecognized and unmanaged system dynamics.

Dis-integration is a painful condition. Chronic dis-integration experiences threaten our emotional and physical well-being. And the personal dramas of organizational Middles can be examined from the perspective of the choices they make as to how to cope with the existence or possibility of dis-integration.

Reactions To Dis-Integration

In this section we will explore some characteristic reactions to the existence or threat of personal dis-integration in the middle. The first pattern, Burn Out, reflects a failure to cope: the Middle remains in a dis-integrated condition until he or she can no longer function in that position. Through the remaining patterns — Satraps, Superadicals, and Bureaucrats — Middles succeed in resolving the dilemmas of dis-integration, but they do so at the cost of the unique power of the Middle. An example of a successful resolution of middleness, one which both avoids dis-integration *and* actualizes the independent power of the Middle will be presented in the following section.

1. Burning Out: Staying Stuck In The Middle

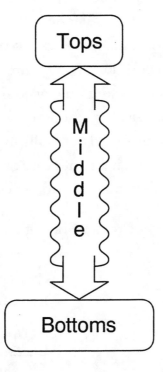

Some Middles remain stuck in the middle. They continue to function as extensions of both Tops and Bottoms; they try to be responsive to both, to be fair to both, and to function as buffers for both. They work very hard, they remain confused and uncertain about a variety of issues, they continue to carry the burden of keeping the system together. They go on being seen by others in the system as hard working, well intentioned, but not as particularly effective people. They continue to work under these conditions until they are no longer able to function to either their own or others' standards. They burn out. They break down physically and emotionally. They are transferred or fired, or they quit the system.

Burn-out occurs when Middles are unable to resolve their dis-integrated condition. In their role as hard working, fair, and responsive extensions of and buffers for both Tops and Bottoms they maintain or worsen this dis-integrated condition until they break down either physically or emotionally. What is the great tragedy of burn-out is that it is often experienced both by the Middle and by others as a *personal* failure. The causes of burn-out are seen as personal, and the treatments, if offered, are personally oriented. Middles are encouraged to jog or stop smoking or exercise or meditate or diet themselves toward greater health. All of these, however beneficial, reinforce Middles' greatest fears: that the problem lies somehow in Middles themselves, that if they took better care of themselves, burn-out would not occur. Burn-out may in fact be related to personal weakness, but it is not only that. It is also a systemic condition, a set of intrapersonal phenomena that are the consequences of unrecognized and unmanaged middleness, and whatever personal weakness may exist — physical or emotional — tends to be exacerbated by those dynamics. Systemic weakness tends to multiply personal weakness; and the solution to burn-out, along with taking better care of oneself, involves understanding and managing the dynamics of middleness.

2. Satraps and Superadicals: Sliding Up and Sliding Down

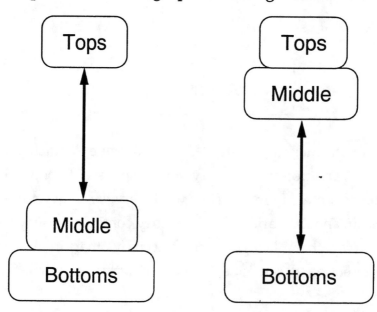

Some Middles resolve the dis-integration of middleness by getting out of the middle. Rather than being extensions of *both* Tops and Bottoms, and rather than being *equally* responsive to both, they align themselves with one or the other. The choice to align oneself upward or downward may be made quickly and clearly at the outset of the relationship or there may be a subtle and gradual drift over time in one direction or the other. In either case, sliding up or down, the dilemma of dis-integration is at least partially resolved.

Such Middles are no longer in the middle. They have redefined their roles. They now see themselves as extensions either of Tops or of Bottoms, but not of both. There is, under these conditions, less confusion and less uncertainty, less wishy-washiness of behavior, fewer doubts about oneself; and the organizational lines are more clearly drawn. There tend to be fewer questions about such Middles' competencies; either Tops or Bottoms tend to be satisfied to have such Middles on "their side," and, although "the other side" may not be happy with their Middles' orientation, they clearly know where these Middles stand. They may be dissatisfied with such Middles' behavior, they may treat such Middles as antagonists, but dissatisfaction and conflict are not necessarily reflections on the Middles' competence.

Sliding up or down are ways of resolving the dilemmas of dis-integration. Such Middles are no longer in the middle with all the pain, doubt, and confusion accompanying that condition. They have a home now, either with the Tops or with the Bottoms. In fact they often outstrip their "allies" in the zeal with which their positions are pursued. Middles who slide up often become Satraps, super organization persons who maintain, support, and enforce the goals, directions, wishes, rules, and structures of the Tops beyond what the Tops themselves consider reasonable or practical. And those Middles who slide down often become Superadicals, outdoing the Bottoms in their zeal for organizational change, in their radicalism, in the intensity of their confrontation of Tops. In either case, as Satraps or Superadicals, Middles do successfully resolve their dilemmas of dis-integration. They are now clear about their position; they know where they stand, but as we shall see, they do so at the sacrifice of middle power. At best they now enjoy the power potential of Tops or Bottoms, but the unique power of middleness is lost to them.

3. Bureaucrats: Non-Responsiveness

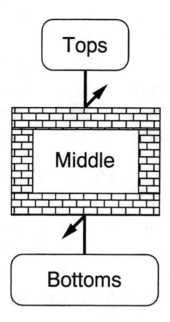

Some Middles resolve their dilemmas of dis-integration by becoming non-responsive to *both* Tops and Bottoms. They see themselves neither as extensions of nor in the service of either. In fact, their tendency is to define *both* Tops and Bottoms as antagonists to be resisted rather than supported. Their tendency is to withhold rather than to provide service. They offer little on their own; they are resistant to requests from others; they create buffers around themselves to discourage intrusions from Tops and Bottoms; they generate complex procedures, forms, and evaluation mechanisms all of which discourage approaches from Tops and Bottoms and all of which make access to middle resources complex, painful, and costly. This mesh of bureaucratic barriers, procedures and complexities does enable such Middles to avoid the dilemmas of dis-integration. Again, the problems of doubt, confusion, and uncertainty are minimized. Such Middles are clear about where they stand and what they do and do not do. There is no frantic rushing back and forth, bearing bad news, putting out fires. There are fewer problems of homelessness, of always transacting one's business in other people's spaces or on the run, for such Middles are firmly entrenched and territorially secure. They have their space, and others come to them when they must. And such Middles have fewer doubts about their own competencies. If there are problems in the system, these Middles are more likely to see the fault as lying with Tops and Bottoms, with their unreasonable requests and demands, with their inability or unwillingness to cope with and manage sensible bureaucratic procedures.

This non-responsiveness to both Tops and Bottoms resolves the dilemmas of dis-integration for such Middles. It does, in fact, create a type of power base for Middles who control resources others need access to and who also control the means of access. But, as we shall see, this pattern of non-responsiveness does deny to such Middles the unique power which comes from the diffusion of middleness.

Power And Powerlessness In The Middle

The power of middleness comes from the diffusion characteristic of the middle space, the fact that Middles are "out there" in the system, that they have contact with Tops and Bottoms and others in the system, that they have the opportunity to see, to interact with and to understand the various sub-worlds existing within the larger world of the system as a whole. In some sense, the greater the diffusion of the position, the greater its potential for power.

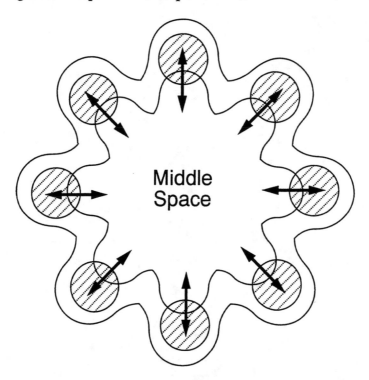

It is this contact with, information about, and familiarity with various pieces of the system which provides Middles with their power. If Middles are able to stay in the middle, to diffuse without dis-integrating, they are in a position to respond sensitively to system issues because of the amount and nature of information available to them about pieces of the system and the system as a whole. And, they are in a position to be proactive as well as responsive, to influence Tops and Bottoms and to influence the way Tops and Bottoms interact with one another.

The challenge for Middles is to be *responsive* to Tops and Bottoms yet *independent* of them, to understand the perspectives of Tops and Bottoms while at the same time clarifying and acting on their own middle perspective, that is to diffuse through the system while at the same time remaining independent and integrated entities within the system.

Whatever else the Satrap, Superadical, and Bureaucratic orientations gain for Middles, these must also be thought of as self-protective mechanisms. By sliding up or down, or by building intricate barriers between themselves and both Tops and Bottoms, Middles protect themselves against dis-integration. In doing so, however, they lose their potential for information gathering, for developing an independent perspective, and for influencing the nature of the interactions between Tops and Bottoms. Middles who remain stuck in the middle maintain their information-gathering capability, but in their unrelenting responsiveness to Tops and Bottoms, they lose their capacity for independent thought and action.

Responsiveness is a central feature of the middle position. It is often what Middles are hired to do. Yet, from a *power perspective*, responsiveness is a means, not an end. It is a process which provides Middles with the information on which an independent middle perspective can be developed and independent middle action can be formulated, and it is this independence which is the key to middle power. By developing an independent position for themselves, Middles are able to diffuse without dis-integrating, and they are able to stay in the middle and use the special opportunities of that position.

The following case describes the growth of a Middle from dis-integration to independence, integration and power. As we shall see, such growth offers new opportunities for Middles both to strengthen their own position within the system and to influence the system constructively. We shall also see that such power is not without its costs, that it creates new dilemmas and new choices for Middles.

Daniel

Part I. Stuck In The Middle And Dropping Out Of New Hope

Early one morning in New Hope, while making my anthropologist's rounds, I spotted Daniel by the swimming pool. He was in his bathing trunks, stretched out on a cabana lounge, covered from head to toe with tanning lotion, a detective novel by his side.

"What are you up to?" I asked.

"Getting some sun."

"Where's the action?" I inquired, vaguely gesturing in the direction of the other New Hope buildings.

"No idea," he answered, his eyes closed as he lay, immobile, on the cabana.

"What about the Elite and the Outs? Weren't you working on some negotiation?"

For this Daniel sat up and, with an edge of anger in his voice, replied, "I've had it with them. I'm finished. As far as I'm concerned THEY CAN KILL ONE ANOTHER." Then, as though that thoroughly covered the matter, he lay back on the cabana and closed his eyes.

THEY CAN KILL ONE ANOTHER. Coming from Daniel that was a remarkable statement. Daniel was a Middle in New Hope and for a number of days he had followed the characteristic middle pattern. He had been hard working, responsive and responsible. He had shuttled regularly back and forth between the Elite and the Outs, bearing messages, mediating, negotiating, cajoling, explaining, and justifying each group to the other, trying to be fair to both, feeling very responsible for keeping the system together and making it work, persevering in the face of abuse from both the Elite, who complained he wasn't doing enough to bring the Outs into line, and from the Outs who regularly accused him of being a "company man," a sellout who failed to deliver on promises, a powerless messenger who couldn't make decisions on his own. Daniel had been seen by both the Elite and the Outs as a hard working, well intentioned, but not particularly effective Middle, and, until now at least, he could always be counted on to work in the best interest of the system. But not now.

THEY CAN KILL ONE ANOTHER. As I left the area, Daniel dove into the pool. Both the Elite and the Outs repeatedly tried to pressure him back into the middle, but Daniel would have none of it.

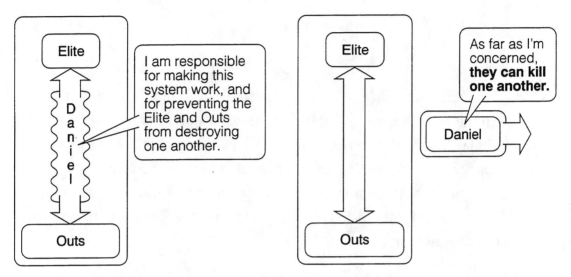

Daniel's action can be viewed as a move toward self-preservation, as a movement away from being swept along by others and toward greater independence, as a movement away from personal dis-integration — confusion, uncertainty, vacillation — and toward greater personal integration — clarity, coherence, strength. What relevance this move has, however, for organizational effectiveness generally, and for middle power specifically, remains to be seen.

Part II: Power in the Middle

Two weeks after the program ended, I got a call from Daniel, and here is his story.

Monday morning, first day back on the job, there was a message for me to call Charlie Smith. URGENT. I called.

"Daniel," he said. "Glad you're back. There's a problem. While you were away, Upstairs sent us our contract for next year, and we don't like it. In fact, it stinks. We want you to straighten it out with them."

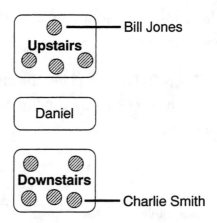

"My God!" I thought. I couldn't believe it. No sooner do I step in the door and there I am back in the middle again. And, from past experience, I know just how this scenario will play itself out: I go downstairs and hear their story, then upstairs and hear theirs, back and forth, getting worn down at both ends, feeling responsible for the whole thing, feeling that it's *my* problem to solve, and catching a whole lot of flak from everyone. Still, I agreed to meet with Charlie and his group to hear what the problems were.

We met. They laid out their problems with the contract and gave me my battle instructions. I told them I wasn't going to do battle for them. They were stunned and started to argue with me. I told them I understood their problems and that I felt that they were entitled to a hearing, but that I wasn't going to do it *for* them.

I told them what I was willing to do: I would try to set up a meeting with Upstairs. I would be at that meeting and I would do all I could to see that Upstairs heard what they had to say. I told them that the contract was *their* problem and *not mine* and that it would be up to them to get their case together and to make their pitch to Upstairs. I told them I would help them plan that process but that I wouldn't do it for them.

The more I talked the clearer it became to me that this was just the way to go. It was not my problem; it was something between Upstairs and Downstairs, and my business was to do whatever I could to help *them* work it out. But Charlie would have none if it; the more I insisted on my plan, the angrier he became.

"No way, Daniel!" he shouted. "You know what the situation is. You work it out with them."

"No way," I replied. "My job isn't to run your errands for you. My job is to help clear this up in the best way possible, and in my judgment, a direct meeting between you and Upstairs *is* the best way."

We tossed it around. They did their best to grind me down, but I wasn't going to be moved. No way was I going to get caught up in that mess again. Finally, more in exasperation than agreement, Charlie threw up his hands. "All right, all right. Set up *your* meeting if you can. But we want to meet with you first to get our act together."

"Fine."

Then I brought the news upstairs to Bill Jones. I summarized the situation for him and recommended the Upstairs/Downstairs meeting. Bill was even more resistant than Charlie, and a tougher game player. He came at me from about five different angles: "We're too busy for that... " "Don't give me any of that human relations stuff... " "It's not cost efficient... " "What do you think we pay *you* for?..." and so on. I hung in there, but Bill flatly refused.

Finally I got him to agree to try it this one time. "Listen," I said, "you pride yourself on your willingness to experiment. Well, let's try this as an experiment and see what happens. It's just one meeting."

"All right," he said, turning back to his work and closing off further discussion. "Set up *your* meeting."

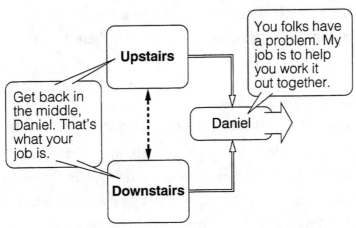

And so we had the meeting, and for the first time in a long time, maybe ever, I felt I was doing my job as it should be done. Upstairs and Downstairs had at one another and I worked as hard as I could to see that they heard and understood one another.

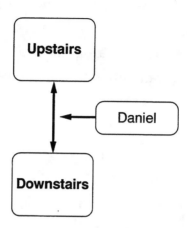

I believe everyone grew some in the process. Upstairs took some of the heat they needed to take; they had been isolating themselves from Downstairs, walling themselves off from things they didn't want to know. And Downstairs grew up a little in their relationships with Upstairs; they took on "the big boys" and nobody died from the confrontation. The meeting was difficult but successful, and the contract problems were resolved satisfactorily.

And I thoroughly enjoyed the whole process. I was the coolest person in the group. When things heated up, mine were the only dry palms in the room. It was clear to me: this contract dispute was not *my* problem; it was something between Upstairs and Downstairs. My business was to make it *possible* for them to work this out. If they could, that would be great. If they couldn't, then it would be all of our responsibility... not just mine.

The System Power of Middleness: Influencing The Patterns of Interaction Between Tops and Bottoms.

Each condition within a system — topness, middleness, and bottomness — offers its unique opportunities for the exercise of *system power*. System power moves are those actions which enhance the *system as a whole*, which improve *its* capacity to survive and develop in its environment. The system power of middleness lies in the possibilities that condition offers us for influencing the patterns of interaction between Tops and Bottoms, for changing those patterns of interaction from less functional forms to more functional ones. Each crisis that develops between Tops and Bottoms offers Middles an opportunity to exercise the system power of their position. A particular difficulty between Tops and Bottoms may be nothing more than an isolated aberration in an otherwise healthy relationship. Oftentimes it is more than that; oftentimes the specific event is symptomatic of chronic interaction problems between the two.

In Daniel's case, for example, the issue for Tops and Bottoms was the resolution of a particular contract dispute. Daniel's move contributed to the resolution of that dispute. Beyond that, however, the specific dispute was used for examining and changing what had been chronic interaction problems between Upstairs and Downstairs: the isolation from each other that both parts were experiencing, the distorted and stereotyped perceptions each part had developed of the other, the arrogance of Upstairs, the counter-dependence of Downstairs, and so forth. When a crisis develops, the agendas of Tops and Bottoms may be limited to resolving the specific issue at hand; for Middles *the specific issue at hand provides the leverage for resolving the core chronic relationship problems between Tops and Bottoms.* That is the system power potential of middleness.

Part III: Power Or Powerlessness In The Middle?

Daniel's story continues:

As the meeting broke up, Bill Jones asked if I would stay on for a minute or two. When the others left, he got up and grasped my hand saying, "Good meeting, Daniel. Productive. Something we all needed." I was feeling terrific. Bill's words simply reinforced my feelings about the morning, and I was eager to get out of there and get some more action going while I was still energized. But Bill didn't let go of my hand. He glanced around the room to be sure that no one was within earshot, then, looking me in the eye, he said firmly "But don't you ever do it again!" I smiled. Bill didn't. It was clear, in that awkward moment, that I had mistaken an order for a joke.

Take What You Want, Says The Lord, And Pay For It.

Old Arabic Proverb

I am often asked to talk to groups or conduct for them some event related to power. When we go into the reasons behind the invitation, it often comes out that some people, generally Middles, feel themselves to have little power in the system and want me to do something to convince those they perceive to have more power to "share their power with others". Their image of shared power generally goes like this: "I want others to let me do what I want to do, to give me permission, and I do not want to have to pay the price for that freedom." It is an appealing dream but one which, I believe, has little to do with power. Power in the middle, as in any system relationship, has its price. The choice for us is to exercise power *and* pay the price or to pass up the opportunities for power and pay the price for that.

Daniel's move was a powerful one. He used the uniqueness of his position. He remained a Middle rather than becoming either a Top or a Bottom. He used his familiarity with and understanding of both Tops and Bottoms to develop his own plan, a middle plan, for what was needed. And, from the outset, that independence was resisted by both Upstairs and Downstairs.

Independence is a difficult condition to develop and sustain within social systems. It is often resisted on the grounds that it is self-serving and potentially destructive to the system, and in many cases it is. In many other cases, however, *independence is neither self-serving nor system-destructive and still it is resisted*. It is a reasonable assumption for Middles to make that if push comes to shove, Tops and Bottoms will be more interested in having Middles serve the local interests of their respective pieces of the system than in serving the interests of the system as a whole. The major challenge for Middles in attempting to realize the power of their position is to cope with the condition of independence, the pressures to come back into line, and to negotiate energetically with Tops and Bottoms to legitimate and maintain that independence.

Daniel tasted the power of middleness and as we left him he was also sampling the costs of that power. The resolution of the dilemma of middleness is not easily made. The costs may clearly outweigh the gains, or they may appear to. That was

Daniel's boss who said "Don't you ever do it again!" Daniel can treat that as another characteristic message to Middles: "You've done something wrong again; you're not measuring up." Or, he can treat it as a signal that the most significant struggle over the nature of his middleness is about to be waged. How willing is Daniel to address the issue? How firm is his boss? How negotiable is the position? How will those below him react? To this point Daniel's move has been a neat trick. A one shot victory, a pilot project, a good story to demonstrate an interesting point. It may remain as simply that. Or it can be the first step in a high risk and continuing venture toward middle power.

Chapter 2

*MIDDLES OF THE WORLD,
INTEGRATE! —*

The middle group

Introduction

The following chapter is based on a speech given in 1982. The focus of culture change at the time was Productivity and Quality of Work Life. But as you will see, though the "hot topic" of organization improvement may change from year to year (Total Quality, Re-engineering, Empowerment), the so-called "middle problem" stays constant. Middles are resistant, Middles won't give up their power, Middles are too weak, too old, too young, they have no added value, and so forth.

In this chapter we take a deeper look at the Middle group, an oxymoron of organization life. At the time, and for the most part it is still true, one did not think of the possibilities of Middle groups; there were worker teams and executive teams, but Middle positions were solitary. Middles connected with Bottom teams (as Coaches for example) or were linking pins to Top teams, but the notion of semi-autonomous Middle groups was, and continues to be, foreign.

Here we shall see how the absence of powerful Middle peer groups has disastrous consequences both for Middles and for the total organization.

In this chapter we introduce the concept of *system power* — that is, the unique power leverage each part of the system (Top, Middle or Bottom) has to enhance the capacity of the system as a whole to survive and develop in its environment. Most culture change efforts focus on enhancing the system power of workers to the neglect of that for Middles (and Tops). The question is: What is the system power of Middles? What is the unique contribution Middles can make to system survival and development? What stands in the way of the development of system power in the middle? And how does one make it happen?

The Middle Manager Dilemma: Too Much Power Or Too Little?

It is interesting that the occasion for this paper is a Quality of Work Life Conference and that I have been invited to speak on "Middle Manager Dilemmas in P/QWL[1] Efforts." What interests me is this: First, that I have had no direct involvement in Quality of Work Life projects and, second, that there has been of late a flurry of activity around me related to such projects. For example:

I. I was contacted recently by an internal consultant from a public utility. The situation he presented was this: His organization is undergoing a Quality of Work Life effort; Middle Managers were the stumbling block; they had to be influenced, he said, *to give up some of their power*. All of this seemed somewhat strange to me. I didn't think Middle Managers *had* much power. *Just what was it they were being asked to give up?*

II. I was conducting a series of workshops for first line supervisors in a manufacturing plant. One day, while walking through the lobby accompanied by a member of Middle Management, I noticed a display describing Quality of Work Life activities in the plant. There were photographs of happy workers, summaries of accomplishments, brightly colored charts and graphs. It looked interesting and potentially relevant to my work. I asked my Middle Manager guide about the project. He seemed uninterested, and tried to hustle me along my way. "Is it relevant to my work?" I asked. He told me it was not. It was someone else's project, he said; it held little interest for him and, he assured me, it was not particularly relevant. My guide was not only a fourteen year veteran of Middle Management, he was an Organizational Development Specialist to boot. If Quality of Work Life activities had so little significance for him, then how important could they really be?

III. When I was invited to speak at this conference, I received this message from one of the program's organizers: "Have Barry Oshry talk about Middle Power. Not shared power. He'll know what I mean." I did not yet know precisely what he meant but I confess that the invitation *not* to talk about shared power — particularly in reference to Middles — had an appealing ring to it.

[1] Productivity/Quality of Work Life

IV. Finally, with two invitations to speak at Quality of Work Life Conferences, I felt that it would be to my benefit, not to mention yours, that I familiarize myself somewhat with the field. Last month I participated in a conference on the subject and paid close attention to a number of reports from the front lines. One stands out. This particular program has been developing for three years; nearly 50 Quality Circles are in place spread throughout manufacturing, quality control and engineering; workers are demonstrating that they can make significant positive contributions to production processes; and, among those workers involved in the Quality of Work Life activities, there are significant reductions in grievances, accidents, product errors, lost time and job turnover. There is one problem, however: the first line supervisors! (My ears pricked up.) Supervisors don't seem to be enjoying the process very much; some are hostile to it; some are dropping out; some are disrupting meetings; and some are even SABOTAGING the effort. When asked what that was all about, the speaker hesitated and then confessed, "We've got a weak supervisory group." (Right about then I knew why I was there!) The speaker elaborated on his problems with supervisors: they're weak; they're young; they don't get along with one another; they aren't skilled enough ("despite *all* the training we give them," he said with some exasperation). The following questions were *not* asked:

▲ Is it your company's policy to *hire* weak supervisors?

▲ Is there some constitutional deficiency underlying weak supervisory behavior? Is the problem *biological* and therefore resistant to "all the training we give them"?

▲ Is there anyone in this audience who can stand up and say: "We've got a *strong* supervisory group. Our Workers see them as strong; our Top Management see them as strong"?

Beware, Middles! They're talking about you again. *You* are the problem; you probably always were the problem; we just never recognized it before. We used to think the Workers were the problem: out for a buck, trying to get away with whatever they could. But we were wrong. See how bright the Workers are, how intelligent, how committed to work and to improving work processes. See how well they work with Top Management and how well Top Management works with them. You, Middles, you're the problem. If only you'd get out of the way, if only you'd let it happen, if only you weren't so weak, if only you'd give up some of your power.

Let me go on record now: Some of my best friends are Middles. Some of the nicest people I know — the hardest working, the most committed to the organization, the most responsible, the most loyal — are first line supervisors and their bosses, and all those who fill the great Middle Management ranks of our organizations.

Watch out, Middles, you're getting a bum rap; and the worst of it is this: some of you are beginning to believe that the problem really is *you*. If enough people tell you you're not up to the challenge, maybe they're right. Maybe a better person could do something. Maybe you need more training. Maybe you're not strong enough. Maybe — God forbid! — you really are incompetent. Forget it, Middles. It's not true. None of it. You're not weak; you're not incompetent; you're not undertrained; and you're not the problem. Holding on to power is not your problem; and giving up your power is no solution. Discovering your power and using it is more to the point.

The points I'd like to make today are these:

1. Quality of Work Life, as I understand it, is basically an empowerment process. The business of Workers is to produce, and Quality of Work Life activities unshackle Workers; they *allow* Workers to produce; they *allow* them to apply their energies to work and to apply their intelligence, expertise, skills and abilities to improving work processes. Quality of Work Life enables Workers to *change their systems*, to influence those systems so that they are better able to do whatever it is they are supposed to do. And that is *power*![2] (I realize that with that statement I may have set back the Quality of Work Life movement ten years because many Top Managers have more zest for what heightens productivity than for what stimulates empowerment; and if they had to choose between more power and more productivity on the one hand, versus less power and less productivity on the other, many have and would continue to opt for less power

---

[2] At the time of this speech, empowerment had not yet attained legitimate status.

and less productivity.) The question is this: Does this empowerment of Workers need to come at the expense of Middle Power? The answer to that will be: NO!

2. The problem is not that Middles must give up their power. They never had any in the first place. Sabotage is not the action of powerful people; it never has been. It is the action of desperate people, of powerless people. The empowerment of Workers comes through producing, through influencing the system by influencing the production process. What is the parallel for our many layers of Middles? How do *they* influence the system? The fact that most of us do not have a ready answer to that question is itself illuminating of the Middle dilemma. What do Middles do? Why are they there? What is their function? What is *their* power?

3. The questions we need to ask are these:

   ▲ What is Middle Power?

   ▲ Why is Middle Power hard to come by?

   ▲ What is the common lot of Middles? What happens to them when they are not empowered?

   ▲ How can Middles become empowered in ways that enhance rather than detract from Quality of Work Life processes?

To explore these questions we will need to step back and examine Middles within the system context in which they function. What does it mean to be powerful in a system? Is power always the same, or does power take different forms depending upon one's position within the system?

What Is Power In Systems And What Is The Power Of Tops, Workers, And Middles?

Power, in its more common usages, raises such questions as: Who controls the resources? Who sits on top of whom in the hierarchy? Who says Yes or No? Who intimidates whom? Who has the fancier working conditions?

The empowerment of Workers in Quality of Work Life activities, however, has come primarily not by changing any of the above but by *creating conditions which allow Workers to influence and improve the workings of the total system.* Quality of Work Life, when it works, is changing the role of Workers in the system. Workers are no longer the children of a system in which all of the important decisions are made by their Top Management parents. Workers are no longer either "good children" who cooperate and do what they are told or "bad children" who resist or rebel; they are adults. They influence not only their own condition but, more importantly, the condition of the system itself. They make IT healthier. It is through their efforts in Quality Circles and other activities that the system is better able to survive in its environment and to develop its potential in that environment. It is through their efforts that the system is better able to cope with the threats to system survival and to prospect in the opportunities waiting to be capitalized on.

This is the first prize of power for all of us who work in systems: *to be able to act in ways which enhance the capacity of our systems to survive and develop in their environments.* When we're able to do that we know we're powerful. If we cannot influence systems this way, then all the other trappings of power — control, dominance, perquisites, intimidation, revenge, hard-lining, bottom-lining — all of these are nonsense; they are power's second prizes (or booby prizes); they are *attempts* to feel powerful or look powerful; they are the consequences of not being powerful. But the true bottom line of system power is this: Are you able to influence the system? Are you able to act in ways which help the system cope and prospect more effectively in its environment? You may be the chief executive of your organization, you may enjoy an astronomical salary and luxurious perquisites, you may be King or Queen of the hill intimidating and dominating all comers, but if you cannot influence the system so that it is better able to cope and prospect, you are working on second prize.

The power we are talking about is System Centered Power — the ability to influence system survivability, the ability to act in ways that enhance system coping and prospecting. Workers have such power — or the potential for such power — by virtue of their control over the processes of work. The work processes themselves provide the unique leverage by which Workers alone can exert that particular form of System Centered Power. Quality Circles and other Quality of Work Life processes create the medium within which that leverage can be exercised. The question remains: What is the equivalent System Centered Power leverage for Middles?

Let us step back and look at Middles (and Tops and Workers) in the system context in which they function. If we were superscientists in the sky looking down on the infinite variety of human social systems, much of what we would see would be some variant on the form below.

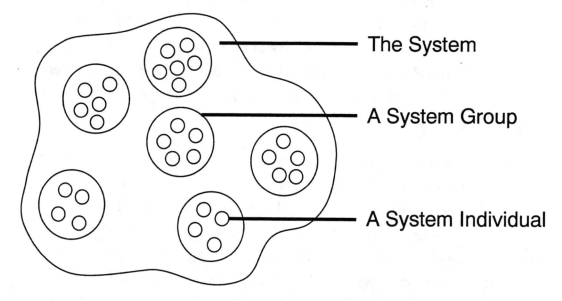

There is an entity existing in its environment. It functions as a whole, and it is composed of parts (individuals and groups). The parts in one sense appear to be autonomous and self-directing entities (exercising free will?) and in another sense they appear to be interdependent, interlocking components of the whole. The system interacts with its environment; it produces products or renders services which are used by individuals or other systems in its environment.

The system exists in an environment that is both dangerous and promising, that presents threats and opportunities. The system *copes* and *prospects*; it protects itself against danger and it takes advantage of opportunities. The system copes and prospects by *managing its form*: by developing variety and complexity of form so that it can cope and prospect in the complexity of its environment, by changing its form to adapt to changing environments. The system copes and prospects by *integrating* the actions of its parts so that parts influence and are influenced by one another; parts enhance one another; parts adjust their performances to the coping and prospecting needs of the whole. And the system copes and prospects by *individuating*: attracting high quality parts, discarding low quality parts, and making good use of whatever parts it has. The power of this system is measured by its capacity to cope and prospect, and how well it does that depends on its ability to manage its form, to integrate its parts, and to use well the parts it has.

Let us look more closely at these system entities. Again, despite the wide variety among them, there is a certain commonality of form.

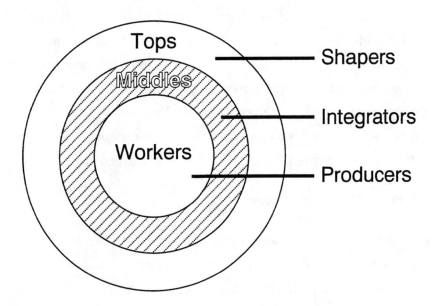

There are various layers to each system: an outer layer (Tops) who run the whole operation, an inner core (Workers) who produce the system's products and render its services, and one or more intermediate layers (Middles) who service or manage various system parts. Each of these layers, by virtue of its position, has its unique system power potential, its own leverage over processes that can enhance the system's capacity to cope and prospect. The system power potential for Tops is to function as SYSTEM SHAPERS, for Workers it is to function as SYSTEM PRODUCERS, and for Middles as SYSTEM INTEGRATORS.

Tops are in the best position to manage the system's overall form: to sense the system's environment, what it is now and how it is changing, to identify the dangers and the untapped opportunities in that environment, and to re-shape the system as needed, sometimes fine-tuning it and sometimes radically overhauling it, so that the system is better able to cope with the dangers and prospect among the opportunities. That is their system power potential.

Workers are in the best position to use their closeness to work and their familiarity with work processes to influence the processes by which work is done in the system, and thereby enhance the capacity of the system as a whole to cope and prospect. That is their unique system power potential.

And the various layers of Middles are in the best position to integrate the system as a whole or various sub-systems within the system. Middles can convey information and materials back and forth among system parts, they can influence system parts so that these parts function in synchrony with one another, so that there is consistency among system parts (when consistency is desirable), so that parts enhance rather than interfere with one another, so that each part can adjust its performance to the coping and prospecting requirements of the system as a whole. And that is the unique power potential of Middles.

Some points about system power:

▲ No one of these forms of power detracts from any other. If Middles integrate the system well, they enhance rather than inhibit the abilities of Tops to shape and Workers to produce; if Tops shape well they enhance the abilities of Workers to produce and Middles to integrate, and so forth.

▲ Although each layer of the system has its unique leverage over system power, no one level can perform its function without the cooperation of other layers. Tops cannot shape systems unless Middles and Workers invest their productive energies in the shapes they develop; Middles cannot integrate systems unless Tops and Workers allow themselves to be influenced by them. Workers cannot produce unless Tops create structures which enable rather than inhibit production.

▲ Shaping, Producing and Integrating are the system power potentials of Tops, Workers, and Middles. In many systems these potentials are only minimally developed; Tops don't shape, Workers don't produce, and Middles don't integrate. Each layer has its unique potential, but each also has its unique dilemmas, and when these dilemmas are not resolved, the power potential goes untapped.

Let us now take a closer look at the unique power potential of Middles and the dilemmas Middles need to resolve for that power to be developed and used.

Middles As System Integrators

Middles need to discover and use their unique system power. Their leverage lies in influencing the integration among system parts.

In this section we describe how Middles would function as System Integrators: what they would do; how their actions would enhance the capacity of the system to cope and prospect; and how this process would enhance the experiences of Middles in systems.

Here we are describing the *possibilities* for Middles, their potential for exerting system power. In fact, few Middle groups function as System Integrators, and in the following section we will explore why this is so.

The Dual Function of Middles: Managers/Servicers and System Integrators

Middles have two functions in the system. One is a *local* function, the other *systemic*.

Middles as Servicers/Managers. The local function of Middles is to service or manage specific system units. This function can be performed *individually*.

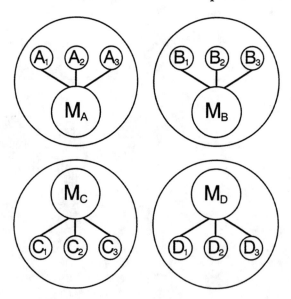

Middles as System Integrators. The systemic function of Middles is to integrate the system (or sub-system). This function can only be performed *collectively*.

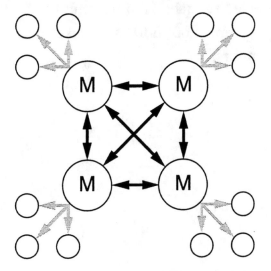

System integration is an appropriate function for Middles; they are in the best position to do it; it empowers them to function as System Integrators and they are disempowered when they do not. In order to integrate the system, Middles must integrate themselves. Let us explore how the process works.

The Integrating Group

The integrating group is a collection of peers within a system. These may be first line supervisors in a plant, corporate staff specialists, store managers in a fast food chain, department chairpersons in a university, school principals in a city-wide school system, senior managers, and so forth.

When it performs its integrating function, the Middle group meets and works without the boss. The boss and others may be invited to participate from time to time when their resources are required by the group. Middle group meetings are separate from staff meetings with the boss; they have different functions and are likely to have different dynamics. Meetings with the boss heighten issues of competitiveness among Middles, dynamics which may be present but less obtrusive when Middles meet alone. Meetings with the boss also tend to suppress openness around problems Middles are experiencing (relationships with the boss may be one such problem area), and meetings with the boss tend to promote dependence rather than independence among Middles: the boss tells us what to do and we submit, resist, or rebel; or we bring our problems to the boss and he or she takes care of them or not. The exclusion of the boss is not an anti-authoritarian act, although it may be perceived as such; it is a structural arrangement promoting the independence and empowerment of Middles; it makes it possible for Middles to function as System Integrators.

The Process Of Integrating The System: Diffusing Outward And Integrating With One Another

Middles integrate the system (or sub-system) by moving back and forth between diffusing out to the system parts they individually service or manage and coming back to integrate with one another.

When Middles are in a *diffusing* phase:

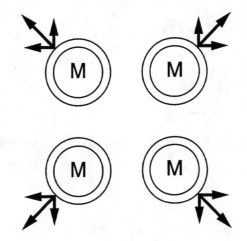

▲ they function independently of one another

▲ each services or manages the specific system parts for which he or she is responsible

▲ each attempts to influence these parts

▲ each collects information about these parts (What do the parts need? What difficulties are people experiencing? What are people's attitudes? What events of significance have occurred? What problem is the Middle experiencing in servicing or managing?)

When Middles are diffusing they have two functions: *influencing* the parts they are servicing and managing, and *data gathering* regarding the life of these parts. (Note that when Middles are diffusing they generally have contacts with a variety of system parts — subordinates, clients, Middles of other levels and functions, and Tops — so that their opportunities for influence and data gathering extend to all of these.)

When Middles are in an *integrating* phase:

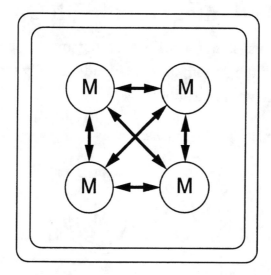

▲ they meet with one another; they exclude all others *including their bosses* (although these may be included from time to time as resources for whatever the group is doing).

▲ they share and make use of the intelligence individual members have gathered while diffusing throughout the system. The potential intelligence pool for a Middle group is considerable; collectively they often have access to more system-wide information than any of the other system parts with whom they have contact, including Tops. This potential is realized, however, only if Middles share their information with one another.

▲ Middles can choose to integrate at a number of levels ranging from "light" involvement with one another to "heavy" commitment to one another. The choice of level of integration has implications for the system power of the group, and for the personal power and individual freedom of its members. (This choice among levels of integration takes on greater significance as we explore issues and processes involved in developing Middle group power.)

▲ Generally, the higher the level of integration, the greater the potential for individual and system power (although Middles might simply jump to organize themselves as as a power bloc and focus on improving their *own* condition within the system without concern for the consequences their demands have for system survival and growth).

▲ It is also true that as Middles move toward higher levels of integration members may feel more constraints on their individual freedom. As the group develops an agreed-upon mission, diagnoses of system-wide issues, and strategies for change, members rightfully expect support and consistency from one another.

▲ *Diffusing and integrating activities strengthen one another.* The more effectively Middle group members integrate with one another — sharing and assimilating information — the more strengthened each individual Middle is in carrying out his or her servicing or managing functions: Middles feel more informed; they have a better sense of the connections among system parts; they feel more secure having a solid data base for their decisions and actions; they feel more in harmony with other Middles. And the more skilled Middles become at gathering intelligence from the field, the richer the contributions they are able to make to the group's integrating activities.

Levels Of Integration

LEVEL 0. **No Integration.** Middles may choose to function as individual operators and not to integrate with one another at all. The personal and system power of such Middles are low, and individual freedom is high in that each Middle is free to act as he or she chooses with no input or constraint from other Middles.

LEVEL I. **Information Sharing.** Middles do nothing more than share information. Each simply puts into the common pool the intelligence gathered from his or her contacts with the system; no analysis is done, no decisions are reached, and each Middle is free to use that intelligence as he or she chooses.

LEVEL II. **Assimilating Information.** Using the pooled intelligence as a basis for system diagnosis. (What trends do we see? What system-wide problems are developing?) Middle commitment to one another is still minimal: they jointly work on system diagnosis but no consensual decisions are made, and each Middle is free to use these diagnoses as he or she chooses.

LEVEL III. **Mutual Consultation.** Using one another as resources to consult on problems individual Middles are facing in their servicing or managing functions.

LEVEL IV. **Joint Planning and Strategizing.** Identifying problems which cut across all Middles' areas of responsibilities and developing agreement among Middles as to how these will be handled. Middles agree to support one another and follow through on their commitments.

LEVEL V. **Power Bloc.** Middles organize themselves as a power bloc within the system, identifying common grievances, needs, and conditions they want changed; they develop bargaining positions and pursue tactics aimed at bringing about the desired conditions.

When Middles function as System Integrators, moving back and forth between diffusing out to the system and coming back to integrate with one another, they are able to function as a significant entity within the system. Even functioning at the lowest levels of integration — sharing and assimilating information — can have major impact on the system and on individual Middles.

Consequences for the System

▲ There is greater consistency throughout the system.

▲ Parts are coordinated with one another.

▲ Tops, Workers, and other level Middles have the information, materials, and directions they need to do their work.

▲ Parts are better able to adjust their performances to the needs of the system as a whole.

▲ And the system as a whole is better able to cope and prospect in its environment.

Consequences for Middles

▲ They feel coordinated and in sync with one another.

▲ They feel supported by one another.

▲ They feel that the Middle group is a significant entity within the system, with a unique mission to perform and the capacity to carry out that mission; they experience group identity and pride.

▲ Each Middle feels more secure and effective in carrying out his or her individual servicing or managing functions; they feel smarter, more knowledgeable about the system.

▲ They feel independent, capable of making their own judgments as to what the system needs.

▲ They feel powerful, able to make things happen in the system.

In summary:

1. The system power potential of Middles is to function as System Integrators — to act in ways which enhance the coordination of system parts, to influence system parts (Tops, Workers, and other level Middles) so that these parts function in sync with one another, so that they enhance rather than block one another, so that each part can adjust its performance to meet the requirements of the whole.

2. Middles have two functions. Their *local* function is to service or manage specific system parts. This function can be performed individually. The *systemic* function of Middles is to integrate the system (or a sub-system within the system). This function can *only* be performed collectively.

3. Middles integrate the system by moving back and forth between diffusing out to the system parts they service and manage and coming back together to share and assimilate the intelligence they have gathered out in the field. When Middles are out in the field, their local function is to influence system parts (through managing and servicing); their systemic function is to gather intelligence about these parts. When Middles are together they integrate with one another at a number of levels ranging from simple sharing of intelligence to developing agreed-upon system diagnoses and action strategies.

4. Middles integrate the system by diffusing out to the system and integrating with themselves. Clearly the bulk of Middle group time will be spent diffusing, being out in the field, servicing and managing, influencing the system parts to which they are assigned; and a much smaller proportion of their time is spent in integrating with one another. Yet, these brief periods of integration can have powerful consequences both for system coordination and for the experiences of individual Middles.

Quality Circles and other Quality of Work Life activities are potentially empowering of Workers. They enable Workers to influence work processes in ways that enhance the capacity of systems to cope and prospect in their environments. It is reasonable for us to demand of Middles that they support such efforts or at least not interfere with them. But that cannot be all we either expect of Middles or offer to them. Middles aren't here simply to help or get out of the way of others. Quality of Work Life involves empowering them as well as Workers (and Tops); it entails helping them discover and exercise their own unique potential for enhancing system survival and growth. There is nothing significant for Middles to give up, only something to find and use.

Why Middles Don't Integrate

Some possibilities:

▲ **Job Definition.** Middles are hired, evaluated, and rewarded as individual contributors. Their jobs have been defined as servicers and managers of other system units and not as system integrators.

▲ **Do Tops Want Integrated Middles?** Many Tops would require an extensive re-education program before they would allow and encourage Middle group integration. Tops need to recognize the potential value to the system of having strong and independent Middle groups which function as System Integrators. Even if Tops recognized the value to the system of Middle integration they might not support something which had the potential for creating new power blocs within the system. Concerns for control might supercede concerns for coping and prospecting. And, finally, the empowerment of another group also raises concerns regarding one's own power or powerlessness. It is, for example, the empowerment of Workers that menaces powerless Middles. Would not the empowerment of Middles menace powerless Tops?

▲ **Do Middles Want Integrated Middle Groups?** Many don't. Of all system groups, Middles are the least oriented toward integration with one another. Middles appear to choose isolation over integration. Middle group members tend to identify more with the groups they service or manage than with their own peer groups. Middle group members tend to have little interest in or zest for mutual collaboration. Relationships among Middle group members tend to be marked by interpersonal tension and competition. Middle group members tend to have little interest in forming a closer and stronger group; they doubt the possibility of forming such a group, and question the potential payoff such a group would have for themselves or the system.

We (and Middles) need to understand these dynamics. Why are Middles the most formidable barriers to their own integration? To answer this question we need to step back once again and look at Middle dynamics and the Middle experience within the context of the larger system.

General System Considerations: Why Tops, Workers, And Middles Don't Use Their Power

▲ The power of a system is measured by its capacity to cope and prospect in its environment.

▲ Each layer of the system has its unique leverage over vital system processes which can enhance the capacity of the system to cope and prospect.

- Tops have the greatest leverage over system form. They can shape the system so that it is better able to cope and prospect.

- Workers have the greatest leverage over production processes. They can influence the processes of work in ways that enhance the system's capacity to cope and prospect.

- And Middles have the greatest leverage over system integration. They can influence system parts so that these parts are in sync with one another, enhance one another, and adjust one another's performance to the coping and prospecting needs of the whole.

Each layer of the system, then, has its unique *potential* for system power: Tops as SHAPERS, Workers as PRODUCERS, and Middles as INTEGRATORS.

▲ Middles are not the only ones who fail to capitalize on their system power potential. Tops often fail to shape systems well, and often they fail to even address issues of system shaping; their energies are elsewhere. And Workers often fail to function as system Producers; their energies too are spent on other matters.

▲ Each system layer has its unique power opportunities, but each also has its unique dilemmas, and if they are unable to resolve successfully these dilemmas, then little of their consciousness or actions are addressed to their system power potential. The unique dilemma for Tops is *complexity*, for Workers it is *vulnerability*, and for Middles it is *diffusion*. Tops who fail to master complexity do not shape systems effectively; Workers who do not resolve their vulnerability in the system fail to produce effectively; and Middles who do not master diffusion do not integrate the system effectively.

- Tops exist in an environment that is more *complicating* than that for either Workers or Middles. The inputs Tops must deal with tend to be more difficult (what isn't resolved elsewhere in the system rises to the Top), more varied, more changing and more unpredictable. Tops, more than others, need special skills in managing complications. When Tops don't manage complications well, their energy is stuck on complications: on not being overwhelmed, on keeping up, staying afloat, fighting fires. And there is little opportunity or inclination to step back from the system, comprehend its current structure, examine the environment and how it is changing, and address themselves to the processes of shaping the system so that it is better able to cope and prospect in that environment. When the day-to-day energy of Tops is spent in fighting losing battles with complications, Tops do not function as system shapers and, what may be more significant, they do not even *see* themselves as system shapers. System shaping is not part of their consciousness: that's not what they do and that's not even a possibility for them.

- Workers exist in an environment that is more *threatening* than that for either Tops or Middles. Workers tend to be more individually vulnerable than others in the system. Generally they are on the receiving end of decisions affecting their lives; they perform under the poorest working conditions; they receive the lowest pay and benefits; they are the most expendable system members, the first to go in hard times. When Workers fail to resolve satisfactorily their vulnerability in the system, then their energies are stuck on self-protection and security: they become docile before authority, submissive, trusting that "goodness" will bring its own rewards; or they become protective, hard-lining, resistant, doing all they can to keep the Tops from influencing them. (What often happens is that Workers fight with one another over whether to be trusting and submissive *or* protective and resistant.) When Workers do not resolve the dilemma of vulnerability, then neither their actions nor consciousness are inclined to producing in the sense we have defined it: actively influencing work processes in ways that enhance the system's capacity to cope and prospect. Not only do Workers fail to produce in this sense, but the concept of themselves as Producers does not exist.

- Middles exist in an environment that is more *diffusing* than that for either Tops or Workers. Middles tend to be pulled away from one another and toward others in the system whom they service or manage. Middles are pulled toward spending their time in other people's territories and not in any common Middle territory. Middles are pulled toward investing their energies in other people's agendas and not in any common Middle agenda. Middles are pulled toward servicing and managing others and not toward giving to and drawing from one another. In short, there are powerful system forces pulling Middles apart, isolating them from one another. When Middles are unable to manage their diffusion, they are controlled by it. (Just as Tops who are unable to manage complications are controlled by them, and Workers unable to resolve their vulnerability are controlled by it.) When Middles are overwhelmed by diffusion, when they allow themselves to be isolated within the system, they do not function as system integrators nor does it enter their consciousness that that is a possibility for them. When Middles are unable to manage their dilemma of diffusion they see themselves not as integrators but as individual managers and servicers, and they view their collection of peers not as a vital system network required for the integration of the system or sub-system but as a collection of individuals each pursuing his or her own path.

In summary,

▲ Tops, Workers, and Middles have unique system power possibilities: Tops as Shapers, Workers as Producers, and Middles as Integrators.

▲ Tops, Workers, and Middles face unique system dilemmas: for Tops it is complications, for Workers it is their vulnerability, and for Middles it is their diffusion. When Tops, Middles and Workers are unable to manage their dilemmas (a) they are unable to capitalize on their system power potential, and (b) they fail to recognize that their power potential even exists.

▲ None of this is inevitable. Tops can be helped to manage their complications more effectively, and when they do they are better able to function as System Shapers. Workers can be helped to manage their vulnerability more effectively and when they do they are better able to function as System Producers. And Middles can be helped to manage their diffusion more effectively and when they do they are better able to function as System Integrators.

▲ Consciousness is shaped by system conditions. When system conditions are changed consciousness is also changed. So long as Middles remain isolated from one another they have one image of who they are and what is possible for them (see below); but once they change their structural pattern of interaction their image of themselves and what is possible for them changes drastically.

The Typical Middle Pattern:
The Exercise Bike Scenario

Most Middle groups do not make the commitment to integration. They do not manage their diffusion; they are instead controlled by it and, as a consequence, the group disintegrates. It gets stuck on diffusion. When this happens there are certain predictable consequences. Consider the following case.

The setting is a chemicals plant. There are four supervisors (M_1, M_2, M_3, M_4) managing their respective units and reporting to a common Top. Workers spend much of their time monitoring various chemical processes, reading dials, and making adjustments as necessary in order to keep these processes under control.

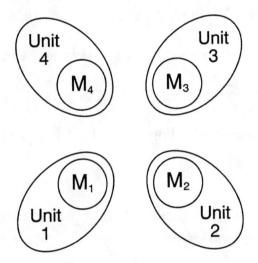

One day the workers in Unit #1 come to M_1 with a request: "How about installing exercise bikes in our area?" The workers make a case that research indicates riding the bikes would not interfere with the accuracy of their readings and, further, that having the bikes would support the company's wellness initiative. M_1 considers the request, finds it reasonable, and makes arrangements to bring in exercise bikes.

Now the predictable story unfolds.

QUESTION: What are the workers in units 2, 3 and 4 now asking?

ANSWER: "Where are *our* exercise bikes?"

QUESTION: And where does M_2 first learn about exercise bikes? From M_1?

ANSWER: "No, from his worker group."

QUESTION: And how is M_2 now feeling about M_1?

ANSWER: "Thanks a lot. Thanks for springing this on me and making me look foolish to my workers."

Meanwhile, M_3 gets the request for exercise bikes from her workers. She thinks it over and decides that it wouldn't work for her operation. "Sorry, no exercise bikes."

Now we have exercise bikes in Unit #1 and no exercise bikes in Unit #3.

QUESTION: How are the workers in Unit #3 viewing the managers?

ANSWER: "Why don't you folks get your act together!"

QUESTION: And how are they feeling about the organization?

ANSWER: "It's not fair!"

And there may be nothing more demoralizing than feeling that you are living in a system in which there is no justice.

Now much of the conversation in the plant is about exercise bikes — do we have them or don't we have them, and what's fair and how screwed up the Middles are.

QUESTION: Where is the issue of exercise bikes now resolved?

ANSWER: "At the top."

So now the issue of exercise bikes comes to the Top who is already burdened with complications, and who is one step removed from the situation.

Next we have committees on exercise bikes. The issue drags on.

Meanwhile, an angry and impatient message comes down from the Top's Top at headquarters. "What's all this business about exercise bikes? I've got important issues that need to be dealt with!"

There are consequences to Middle dis-integration, some of which are depicted in this case. There are more. There are costs for the system, for the Middle group, for how Middles experience themselves, and for how they are seen by others.

Consequences for the System

▲ The system is unintegrated. Not only are Middles isolated from one another but so are the various units they service and manage.

▲ People in each of these units function independently of people in other units.

▲ People tend to be unaware of the connections between what goes on in their part of the system and what goes on in other parts.

▲ People tend to be non-cooperative and often competitive with one another.

▲ Parts tend to be out of sync with one another; they fail to adjust their performances to the requirements of other parts and to the requirements of the system as a whole.

▲ There is inconsistency among system parts causing problems both for people in these parts and for Middles. ("Why are we being treated differently from others?")

▲ There is unnecessary and unproductive duplication of effort.

▲ Middles fail to integrate the system, and problems of integration fall to Tops (thus heightening the complications Tops must deal with and decreasing the likelihood of their functioning as effective System Shapers). This is such a common phenomenon that people often assume that integration is the appropriate business of Tops even though Middles are better situated to do this.

▲ The system as a whole is less integrated than it could be and it copes and prospects less effectively than it would were Middles functioning as System Integrators.

Consequences for the Middle Group

▲ There tends to be no Middle group which functions as an independent unit within the system. Middles may have periodic meetings with their common boss but these meetings have dynamics quite different from those when Middles meet alone.

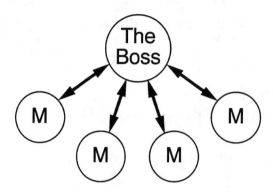

• There tends to be considerably more up and down interaction (and often more down than up) than lateral interaction.

• Middles are less likely to share their common problems in the presence of the boss. (Not to mention that some of their common problems may be with the boss.)

• The presence of the boss heightens competition among Middles.

• The presence of the boss heightens dependency reactions with Middles looking to the boss rather than to themselves for the solution of their problems.

▲ Middles have little interest in or zest for mutual collaboration.

▲ Middles fail to identify or work on common problems.

▲ Middles tend to feel and act competitively toward one another.

▲ Middles often experience interpersonal tension with one another.

▲ As a collection, Middles tend to send inconsistent messages out to the various groups they service or manage.

▲ Middles look to authority for direction.

▲ Middles have little interest in developing a more integrated group and see little or no potential power in such a group.

Consequences For How Middles Experience Themselves In The System

When Middles fail to integrate themselves, they set themselves adrift; they cut themselves off from system information and from opportunities to clarify system dynamics. Middles choose to isolate themselves, but they also pay the price for that isolation.

▲ Middles tend to feel unsupported and sometimes undermined by one another.

▲ Middles often feel insecure as to the validity of their actions, not having enough information to feel comfortable that they are doing the right thing.

▲ They often feel uninformed, surpriseable, that others know things before they do.

▲ They tend not to have independent positions on issues that divide those above them from those below them.

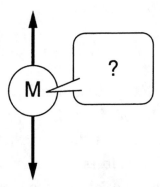

They often feel torn between the two: sometimes aligning with those above, sometimes with those below, sometimes feeling shredded between the two sides.

▲ They feel reactive to what others want and not proactive.

▲ They feel unimportant in the system, like telephone wires or messengers.

▲ They feel responsible for problems they cannot change.

▲ They feel powerless. They have no sense of what their own power in the system is. They exist on borrowed power: some align themselves with their bosses and become extensions of them; some align themselves with Workers and become their champions in the battle against the bosses. Some go after the second prize of power: domination, intimidation, control. But they tend not to have any real power — system power — of their own.

Consequences For How Middles Tend To Be Seen By Others In The System

Middles tend to be seen by others as responsible people who mean well and who try hard; but they also tend to be seen as:

▲ uninformed

▲ wishy-washy, having no clear position of their own

▲ agents of the Top

▲ inconsistent

▲ weak and often incompetent

▲ powerless, unable or unwilling to make important decisions on their own.

Middles find their power by integrating themselves and thereby integrating the system or sub-systems. When Middles fail to integrate, the system suffers, the relationships among Middles deteriorate, and the experiences of individual Middles are unsatisfactory. When Middles recognize that their problems are systemic they will also realize that the solutions to these problems are systemic. The system solution is this: Middles, integrate yourselves and your systems; your systems will be the better for it, your relationships with one another will improve and take on a new meaning, and you will feel stronger, more effective, and more powerful in your work.

But Middles tend not to view their problems systemically. They personalize them. If they are having troubles with their peers they attribute this to an unfortunate mix of personalities and not to the consequences of their systemic condition. Consultants often collude in this. They find a Middle group marked by interpersonal tension and competition. They assume that the tensions and feelings are the causes of Middle group problems. They assume that the way to develop stronger Middle groups is to resolve these tensions and problems. And these assumptions often lead to painful and unproductive interactions and confrontations among Middles, many of whom have little interest in either developing a stronger Middle group or resolving their tensions with one another. When Middles recognize and accept their role as System Integrators, when they integrate with one another as a means for making this happen, then these feelings, tensions and conflicts diminish and often disappear without anyone addressing them directly. The problem is systemic and not personal, and the solution is systemic and not personal.

This also holds true for how Middles experience themselves. When Middles fail to integrate, the Middle position tends to be a stressful one. Middles are isolated, unsupported; they are working in other people's territory on other people's agendas; they are working with insufficient information; they are torn between the conflicting demands, perceptions, and priorities of those above them and those below them; they are not only unsupported by their peers, they are often undermined by them; they try to please everyone and often please no one. It is not unusual under such conditions for Middles to feel stressed, to feel weak and helpless, powerless, incompetent. And Middles often personalize these feelings; they blame themselves, not their systemic condition. ("A better manager could handle this." "If only I were smarter, stronger, more competent.") When Middles personalize the problem they also personalize the solution; and again they are encouraged by others in this: to jog themselves toward greater competence, to diet, to exercise, to meditate, to undergo counseling, training, therapy, and so forth. But the problem is not personal; it is systemic. And the solution is systemic. When Middles integrate themselves and the system then much of the stress and self-doubt simply disappear.

The trick in all of this is to see the middle condition systemically, to realize that the reality that dis-integrated Middles experience — as powerful and as solid as it seems to them — is not the only possible reality available to them. They need to see the possibilities of middleness, to understand the dynamics of the middle position, and to recognize that their current "reality" is merely a consequence of those dynamics. Change the dynamics, master the dilemma of diffusion, and a new reality will appear.

Elements In The Empowerment Of Middles

1. **Consciousness Raising.** The one way not to integrate Middles is to begin by asking them if they want to integrate. Your best prediction is: they won't want to do it. They won't see it as possible; they won't be attracted to the idea of working more closely together; they won't see it as appropriate to their position to "organize"; they won't see its relevance or potential for themselves or the system. We know that these feelings are *consequences* of the dis-integrated state of Middles, but to Middles these feelings are reality: how things are and how they can be. Before Middles can want to integrate, before they can see the possibilities of integration, they must first understand how their current systemic condition shapes their consciousness. This paper is one step toward raising middle consciousness; systems exercises in which the common and predictable dilemmas of middleness can be demonstrated are another step; communication networks among Middles from the most diverse institutional and organizational settings represent still another. When the light first dawns for Middles, when they see the generality of their condition, when they see that you understand their condition without their even talking to you about it, the first reaction is one of great relief. ("It's not just me! It's not just my problem. It's everywhere!") That first phase is significant, but not sufficient. As Middles come to understand the systemic nature of their condition, they may simply use that understanding as an excuse for their weakness. ("What do you want from me; I'm a Middle.") What Middles need to be confronted with is this: if the problem is systemic, so is the solution. Are Middles willing to take responsibility for improving their own conditions? With that question the work begins.

2. **Choosing Among Levels of Integration.** As Middles begin to integrate they need to make decisions regarding the level of integration at which they will function. Concerns about individual freedom versus group control are usually central at this point. Middles are accustomed to operating as loners; it is a source of weakness in the position but it also has its benefits: Middles feel free to handle their position as they choose. Some Middles have strong negative feelings toward collective action with its images of unions, communism, worker cliques, or mindless masses under the spell of Big Brother. I generally recommend that Middles start at the lowest level of integration: information sharing; that they

simply meet periodically to pool the information each has gleaned from his or her contacts with the system, and that there be no commitment to common action. With Level I Integration all Middles are free to use this information as they choose. Level I Integration is by itself a powerful move: Middles feel strengthened, more informed; their day-to-day business is embedded in a larger systems context; and they are still free to act however they choose. As Middles begin to reap the benefits of Level I Integration, they may choose to move up the Integration ladder: assimilating information, diagnosing system-wide issues, using one another as resources to consult on problems individual Middles are facing, or identifying system-wide problems and developing strategies for resolving these. Middles may initially be concerned with coercion by a Middle group and loss of individual freedom. Integrating initially at Levels I and II (Information Sharing and Assimilation) should minimize these concerns. But there is another issue. The emphasis on maintaining one's individuality and concerns for themselves becoming too closely enmeshed in the working of any group may themselves be symptoms of the dis-integrated condition of Middles. Many members of Out groups (who may be seen by In group members as a mindless herd) do not feel that their individuality or freedom is menaced by group involvement; in fact they find that these are enhanced. To some extent the issue of individuality versus solidarity is a political one, and where you come out on the issue is influenced by where you stand in the system. As Middles move up the scale of Integration they may find that their freedom as well as their power is enhanced, that they are not only strengthened by their group membership, they are liberated by it.

3. **Consciousness Raising for Tops.** The empowerment of Middles can proceed with or without legitimization by Tops. In the one case, Tops can recognize the value to the system of integrated Middle groups and legitimate the functioning of Middles as both servicers/managers and system integrators. Or, in the absence of such legitimization and support, Middles might simply choose to integrate themselves and deal with the resistance they would generate among Tops. The former would be a smoother path; the latter would be rockier, but it is possible and in the end might cement closer relations among Middles.

There are two elements to enlisting the support of Tops. The first is rational, the second more emotional. Tops need to see the value to the system (and to themselves) of Middles functioning as integrated groups. They need to be clear about the possibilities of Middles — the function they can serve in the system; they need to be clear about the dynamics of Middleness — the dilemmas Middles face which make it difficult to function or to even think of themselves as potential system integrators; they need to be clear about the costs to the system and to Middles when Middles do not integrate; they need to understand the concept of levels of integration (that middle integration is not the same as unionizing); and they need to understand the mechanisms by which effective integration can take place. To achieve this all that is required is a rational education program for Tops: papers to be read, presentations, analyses of system dynamics, and so forth. For some Tops this may be enough; their primary focus is on shaping the system so that it can cope and prospect more effectively in its environment, and re-defining the role and function of Middles may strike them as a sensible and valuable way of re-shaping the system. For other Tops, rationality will not be sufficient; you may make the case that middle integration is good for Middles and good for the system, and they will still resist it.

Let me tell you a story. Some time ago we were conducting a workshop, the goal of which was to help people understand the dynamics of systems and to focus specifically on the system power opportunities of Tops, Middles, and Workers. The program was four days long and each day we created an organization simulation in which some participants functioned as Tops, others as Middles, and others as Workers. And each day we shuffled the players around: one day you might have been a Top, the next day a Middle, and so forth. In the first exercise, the typical middle pattern developed: Middles were seen as weak, confused, powerless; they dis-integrated as a group; they felt like powerless messengers in the system, reactive rather than proactive, ineffective and incompetent. On the second day a new batch of Middles came on the scene determined to do a better job. They didn't; the middle pattern occurred again despite their good intentions. On the third day still another group moved into the middle position, and this time they decided to attack the middle dilemma systemically. Their plan was this: Each simulation runs for seven "days", but a "day" is only fifteen minutes long. The

Middles decided to do two things: first, they would meet together during the first two minutes of each day and, second, during these meetings they would integrate at the lowest level, that is, simply share information that each of them had gathered during the preceding day. The Middles stuck to their "daily" two-minute information-sharing meetings despite considerable pressure from Tops and from Workers, both of whom had their own demands on middle time.

This simple systemic re-arrangement had considerable impact on the system and completely altered the Middle experience. Middles not only integrated themselves but they effectively integrated the system. Tops and Workers agreed that Middles were the most significant power entity in the system, that they made the whole thing work. Middles were seen as strong, powerful and effective. Middles felt good about themselves, they felt good about their relationships with one another (although they never spent any time working on these relationships), and they felt identity with and pride in their Middle group. All of this from a two-minute daily meeting with Level I Integration.

The system worked well, but not all Tops were happy with this. The fact that the system worked well was not enough. Middles had felt powerful, they had been seen as powerful, and they acted powerfully. But none of this was true for Tops. The system had functioned well in spite of the Tops (although some Tops maintained that the Middle success only happened because Tops had allowed it to happen; this was true but of little consolation). Tops were experiencing a dilemma similar to the dilemma of Middle Managers in Quality of Work Life programs. On the one hand you see the empowerment of others and recognize that they and the system are the better because of it; on the other you wonder about yourself. It is not enough that others in the system and the system itself are doing better. What about you? What is your role? The empowerment of Workers sharpens the powerlessness of Middles. This is not a new powerlessness; it was always there. But it is easier to be powerless in a system in which everyone is powerless than to be in one in which others are powerful and you are not.

The empowerment of Middles will create similar dilemmas for Tops. It will not be enough for them to demonstrate that it's good for the system. The empowerment of Middles will raise questions for Tops: What is our power? What are we doing here? And just as the empowerment of Workers is held up by the powerlessness of Middles, so will the empowerment of Middles be held up by the powerlessness of Tops. All of this, though painful at times, is potentially for the good. As Middles begin to struggle for power, Tops may become the new "bad guys", just as in Quality of Work Life Programs, Middles are now the "bad guys", and as Workers were once the "bad guys". Pointing the finger at Tops is as much nonsense as pointing it at Workers or Middles. Each layer has its potential for system power: Tops as Shapers, Workers as Producers, and Middles as Integrators; and each layer has its dilemmas which stand in the way of that power. When Tops or Middles or Workers cannot work out their dilemmas, they all look like bad guys; when they do work out these dilemmas they don't look so bad anymore. The empowerment of Workers, by sharpening the powerlessness of Middles, may provide the impetus for empowering Middles; and the empowerment of Middles as System Integrators may stimulate the empowerment of Tops as System Shapers. No one of these forms of power is in conflict with any other. They all contribute to enhancing the capacity of the system as a whole to cope and prospect in its environment.

Chapter 3

CONVERTING MIDDLE POWERLESSNESS TO MIDDLE POWER —

Mastering the middle space

Introduction

As we unravel the pitfalls and possibilities of middle positions, it becomes clear that the "middle question" is but a piece of a larger challenge, the challenge of system literacy.

We are systems creatures; our consciousness is shaped by the nature of the system conditions in which we exist. For the most part, however, we are illiterate regarding systems — we do not see systems and we are unaware of the effects they have on our consciousness. As a consequence, we are at the mercy of system processes. Put us into certain systemic conditions, and when things go predictably wrong — with us or with our relationships with others — we fix the wrong things. We focus on fixing people rather than helping people see, understand, and master the systemic conditions in which they exist.

The good news is this: We can do better. Once our focus shifts from fixing people to mastering the space, a whole other domain of strategies begins to emerge.

Are Middles Our Modern Day Witches And Demons?

We are in the Dark Ages of organizational understanding. In the years ahead we will be mocked for the primitiveness of our beliefs just as we now look condescendingly upon those who in great earnestness hung witches. In those dark days, when things went badly, people had their witches to blame; when things go badly for us in our organizations, we have our demons. They had their evidence, we have ours. They hung or burned their witches, we rotate our demons or fire them or humiliate them or hang them out to slowly twist in the wind. Looking back on the witch burners from our "modern day" perspective, we see how bizarre their beliefs were. When future "moderns" look back at us, what will they see?

When things go wrong in our organizations, we see demons. We point the finger at particular people — they are the ones we blame, and they are the ones we "fix" or replace or fire.

Yet many of these demons are as innocent as the witches of yesteryear. You say "Not so" — all the evidence of your senses tells you that these people are in fact the culprits. And I say "Welcome to 20th century witchcraft."

Proust suggests that "the voyage of discovery rests not in seeking new lands but in seeing with new eyes." Which is precisely what we need — a new set of lenses for looking at organizational behavior. With the right lenses, our demons will disappear.

The Missing Lens

Like you, I am a primitive person living in the Dark Ages of organization behavior. My lenses are as primitive as yours. But over the past thirty years I have had the privilege of observing many hundreds of organizations. Some of these organizations are like the ones you work in and are familiar with, others are simulations we have created for purposes of education and research. I have seen things that give me a glimmer into what is missing — the lens we don't have.

What strikes me most about organizations is their regularity — the same scenarios keep happening again and again in the widest variety of settings — manufacturing, high technology, religious institutions, schools, community groups, government agencies, universities. The same patterns keep showing up, but rarely do people feel that they are living out a pattern. Each event seems very specific to their unique organization, circumstances and people. It matters little that all over the world many thousands of people in all varieties of organizations are having the very same experience.

The lens we are missing is a systemic one. We don't see systems, we just see people. We don't see system spaces, we see only the effects these spaces have on us. So when things go wrong, we blame what we see — the people, our demons.

The Middle Space

In this paper we direct our attention to the Middle Space. A Middle Space is a space that pulls us between others. Whoever enters a Middle Space is caught between the conflicting agendas, perspectives, priorities, needs, and demands of two or more individuals or groups. Some Middle Spaces exist between contending vertical pressures (for example, supervisors between their managers and their work groups); others exist between lateral pressures (for example, a liaison between customers and producers); and many Middle Spaces have multiple contending forces vertically and laterally. Supervisors in plants and offices exist in Middle Spaces, as do department chairpersons and deans in universities, middle managers, heads of medical departments, union stewards, and people occupying the many hundreds of other positions in the widest spectrum of organizations and institutions. [In our analyses we will for the most part limit our discussion to the relatively simple Middle Space between Above and Below.](See figure 1)

All of these are Middle Spaces. Some spaces are more middle than others — the greater the differences between Above and Below in perspective, priorities and needs, the more powerful the middleness of the space.

Put people into a Middle Space and there is a story that develops with great regularity. The story varies from situation to situation, but the basic pattern is the same. It is a story of gradual disempowerment in which reasonably healthy, confident and competent people become transformed into anxious, tense, ineffective and self-doubting wrecks. And when this happens we see these persons as our demons — it's too bad we're stuck with such weak and ineffective Middles; fire them or fix them or rotate them or let them swing slowly in the wind.

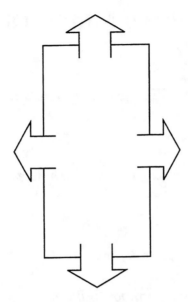

Figure I. The Middle Space—A Space That Pulls Us Between Others

The question is: If we look at these many different Middle stories through a systemic lens, what new understanding and what new strategies for empowerment open up for us?

The Familiar Story Of Middle Disempowerment

"Middles live in a tearing world.

It is a world in which people are pulling you in different directions;

Tops have their priorities and they expect your support;

Bottoms have their priorities — which are generally different from Tops' —

and they expect your support;

Tops want you to get production out of Bottoms

but you can't do that without the cooperation of Bottoms;

Bottoms want you to deliver on their needs and wants

but you can't do that without the cooperation of Tops.

When Tops and Bottoms are in conflict, one or the other or

both try to draw you in on their side.

You please one,

you displease the other;

you try to please both

you end up pleasing neither."[1]

Life in the Middle space is hectic. You are always on the go. So much to do — for everyone — so little time. You spend your time working in other people's spaces and on other people's agendas. You feel squeezed. Tops are distant and remote; they're on another, less tangible wave length, talking about strategy and planning and organization. Meanwhile Bottoms are looking to you for concrete direction and support, but you don't have the direction and support to give to them. You see the attitudes of Bottoms deteriorating and can't do anything about

[1] B. Oshry, **The Possibilities of Organization**, Power & Systems, Boston, 68-69, 1992.

it. You feel useless, like a conduit simply carrying information back and forth. You spend your time going back and forth between Top and Bottom, explaining one to the other, justifying one to the other. There are lots of opportunities to let people down, and few opportunities to succeed. Tops don't seem to move your world ahead; they just give you more work and more uncertainty. You feel like a ping pong ball and Tops and Bottoms are the paddles. You are confused. (In the Middle Space, if you're not confused it means you're not paying attention. You talk to Tops and they make sense; you talk to Bottoms and they make sense too. It's hard to figure out what you believe.) Your actions are weak, compromises, never quite strong enough to satisfy Tops or Bottoms. Sometimes you feel important yet insignificant — as a telephone wire is important, but the real action is not with you, it's on either end of the line. You take a lot of flak from Bottoms, and never feel you can give it back (it wouldn't be managerial). For some reason you feel like it's your responsibility to keep this system from flying apart. Yet much of the time you feel invisible — when Tops and Bottoms are together they talk as if you're not even there. You feel inadequate, never doing quite enough for Tops or Bottoms, never quite measuring up to the job. In time, you begin to doubt yourself — maybe there is something wrong with you, maybe you're not smart enough or strong enough, maybe you're not as competent as you thought. And others in the organization mirror this impression. They see you as a nice person, trying hard, acting responsibly, maybe even well-intentioned. It's just too bad you're so weak and ineffective. Well, maybe with a little more training or meditation or aerobic exercise or therapy or a better diet…

Primitive, primitive! There are no demons here. This is not a personal story; it's a space story. The solution lies not in fixing people but in seeing and mastering the Middle Space.

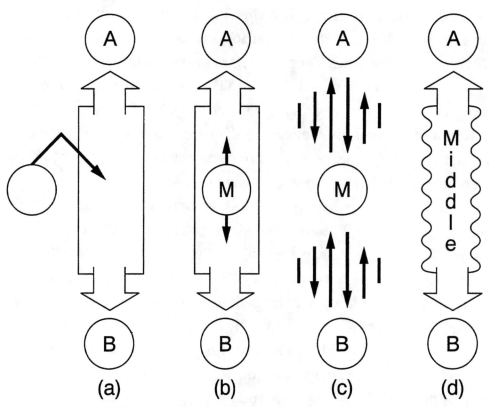

Figure 2. From Healthy to Torn. (a) A perfectly healthy, happy and competent person about to enter the middle space between Above (A) and Below (B); (b) Middle enters the space and attempts to be responsive to both A and B; (c) Life becomes hectic; (d) Middle becomes torn — confused, weak, loses independence.

A Systemic Look At How We Fall Into Disempowerment In Middle Positions

Our methods of preparing people for Middle positions are primitive. We promote them on the basis of dimensions which may be totally irrelevant to their ability to master middleness. We train them on the technical aspects of the job. At best, we offer them leadership or supervisory training — which is Top's way of telling Middle how to handle Top's agenda, but which leaves Middle totally unprepared for the fact that Bottom has its own agenda for Middle in relation to Top.

No dean, no supervisor, no department chair, no section head should enter such a position without first understanding the dynamics of middle positions and learning how to master the Middle Space.

There is a process that happens to us with great regularity when we enter the Middle Space, and this process lies at the heart of our disempowerment as Middles. Simply put, the process is this: We slide into the middle of other people's issues and conflicts and make these issues and conflicts our own. Once we slide into the middle, we are torn.

Objectively, even in middle positions, we are not torn until we put ourselves into the position to be torn. Objectively, Above has its agenda for Below, and Below has its agenda for Above. In that nano-second before sliding in, Middle could be relaxedly observing, "Isn't it interesting the conflicts *they* are having with one another? What's it got to do with me?"

That moment never happens or, if it does, it is too brief. As Middles, we slide into the middle and become torn between Above and Below. In that torn condition we feel that it is *our* responsibility, and our responsibility alone, to resolve their issues and conflicts. Our self-esteem now rests on their evaluations of how well we satisfy them.

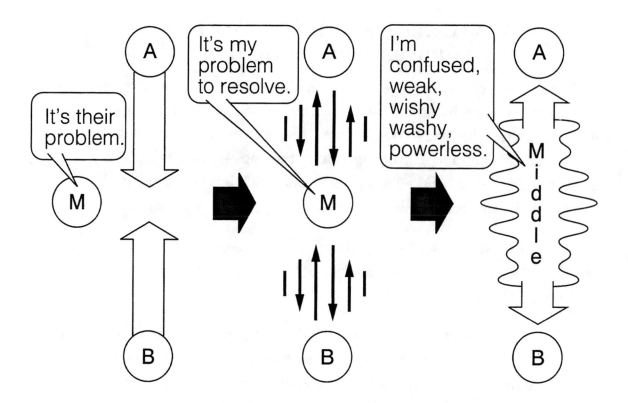

Figure 3. We slide into the middle of other people's issues and processes and make them our own.

This "sliding in" process is not a conscious choice we make. It is more like a reflex. We don't do it, it happens to us. We see a conflict between others, and we feel the full weight of that conflict resting on our shoulders.

> Charlie complains to me, his supervisor, that the shower is not working. In a flash, I'm feeling that it's my fault that the shower is not working and that it's my responsibility to get it working. When I don't get it working fast enough because I can't get the approval from upstairs or because maintenance has this huge backlog, Charlie gets on my case, and I'm feeling weak and foolish and ineffective.

> Louise has been called in to manage a meeting between Above and Below. This is an important meeting; Above and Below have a number of issues between them. Louise is very nervous; she feels that her success or failure rests on how well this meeting turns out.

If Charlie's supervisor or Louise had their systemic lenses on, they might see something else — a flashing sign: "Middleness — Beware of Sliding into the Middle!" And they might pause to consider if there might not be some more powerful way to handle this situation.

Coaching For Middleness:
Two Strategies And Five Tactics For Empowering
Yourself In The Middle

In the absence of a systemic lens, we see only specific events, specific circumstances, specific people — our demons — and we react. With a systemic lens, we see middleness, and that seeing opens up for us new strategies and tactics for mastering the middle space.

Strategy I: Don't slide into the middle of their issues and conflicts and make them your own.

That is, at all times, be clear that this is not *your* problem. *They* are having an issue with one another. Do what you can to empower them to resolve their issues. Resist all efforts on their part to pull you into the middle; the pressures can be quite strong. Understand that Above and Below don't mind at all having you feel responsible for resolving their problems.

Strategy II: Do not lose your mind.

The Middle place is an easy place to lose your mind — *your* view, *your* thoughts, *your* perspective on what needs to happen. When we are torn, our attention is on Above and Below — what they think, what they want, what will satisfy them. In that Middle space, however, we are in a unique position to formulate our own vision of what needs to happen. Generally it is the conflicting information that comes at us from Above and Below that confuses us and causes us great stress. That conflicting information, however, can also be the source of our unique strength. We need to seek that information out — rather than run from it. We need to allow it in and use it to formulate our unique Middle perspective.

With these two general strategies in mind, we can explore specific tactics by which we empower ourselves and others from the Middle position.

Tactic 1: Be Top When You Can, and Take The Responsibility of Being Top.

Sometimes we beg for trouble, and then complain when we get it. In certain situations we make ourselves Middle when we could be Top. Two Middles walk away from a meeting with Tops. One Middle says to the other, "Say, we didn't ask them if we could do (such and such). Let's go back and ask." The second Middle says, "We didn't ask, and they didn't tell us. So why don't we decide what needs to happen. If they don't like it, they'll tell us." The first Middle is uncomfortable with this; he wants to go back, to be in the middle, to find out what they want, to ask permission. The second Middle is uncomfortable with going back; she wants to go ahead, she wants to be Top, to figure out what she thinks needs to happen, to do it, and, if it turns out poorly, to ask forgiveness.

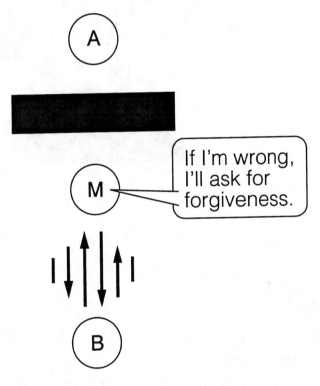

Figure 4. Be Top when you can.

Tactic 2: Be Bottom When You Should.

Middles sometimes describe themselves as "sewer pipes" — "Any garbage that Tops send us we simply pass along to Bottoms... without question." Middle passes the garbage along to Bottom; Bottom complains about the garbage; Middle justifies the garbage, explaining that it's really good stuff; Bottom still sees it as garbage and continues to complain; Middle passes these complaints along to Tops; Tops explain to Middle how the garbage really is good stuff and chastise Middle for not doing a good enough job convincing Bottoms; and on and on it goes. Middles, if they haven't lost their minds, are often in a better position than Tops to recognize garbage as garbage. Don't just be a mindless funnel. Be bottom. Work it out with Tops. The buck stops at the Top; the garbage stops in the Middle.

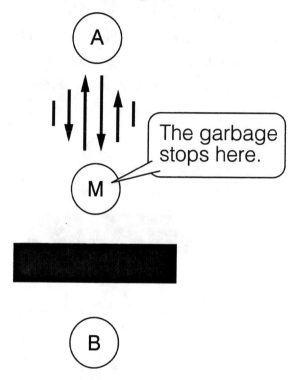

Figure 5. Be Bottom when you should.

Tactic 3: Be Coach.

When others bring their complaints to Middles, Middles assume that it's their job to handle these complaints — which is precisely what it means to slide into the middle. Middles feel ashamed if they still haven't fixed some lingering complaint; they feel embarrassed to admit that all their efforts to date have failed; they feel guilty about not having got around to it; they feel weak and inadequate for not being a more powerful, more effective, more competent Middle. Why all the shame, guilt and self-doubt, Middle? It's not your problem. They're the ones with the complaints. This doesn't mean that you are to be callous, unsympathetic, unfeeling; nor does it mean that you have no important role to play. People have problems. Let them know that you understand their situation, that you empathize with their condition, and that you are not going to solve their problem for them. That's not your job. Your job is to empower others to solve their own problems. Offer to be their coach — to work with them, to empower them so that they can do what they need to do to solve their problems.

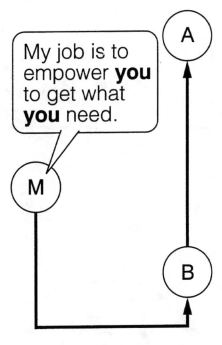

Figure 6. Coach.

Tactic 4: Facilitate.

In the Middle we often find ourselves running back and forth between people, carrying messages from one to the other, explaining one to the other. We learn from the Customer what the Customer's needs are; we carry this information to the Producers; the Producers have questions which we then bring back to the Customer; and then we carry the Customer's answers — along with a modified set of requirements — back to the Producers; and on and on it goes, sliding into the middle. When we are in the middle of such a process, we are harried but with a sense of the importance of our role — we are needed by both sides. When we are caught up in this process, it may never occur to us to ask: why am I doing all this running? Why not step out of the middle, bring together those people who need to be together, and do whatever it takes to make their interaction with one another as productive as possible?

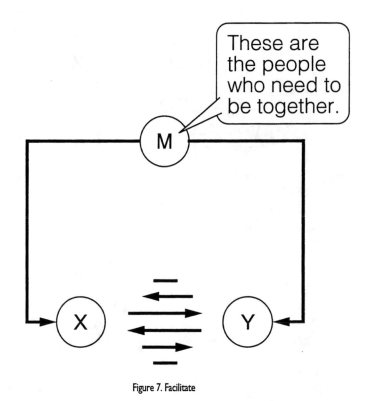

Figure 7. Facilitate

New options open up for us when we see situations systemically. Our interactions in organizations are not simply people interacting with people — isolated events in unique circumstances. People always interact with one another in systemic spaces. When we are blind to the effects of these system forces, we invite the space to disempower us. When we see systemically, we understand the space, we know what it can do to us, and we know what challenges we face in mastering the space.

Tactic 5: Integrate With One Another

There is another factor that relates to the power and contribution of Middles, and that has to do with the nature of Middles' relationships with one another. Middles strengthen themselves and enhance their contributions to their organizations by developing strong peer group relationships — among supervisors, among deans, among section heads, among plant managers, among department heads. Yet such relationships rarely develop. For most people the term Middle Group is an oxymoron — if it's a group then it can't be Middles, and if there are Middles, it can't be a group. Middles, left to their own devices, do not become teams, they do not develop powerful and supportive relationships with one another. They generally resist all efforts at team development. This alienation from one another is a major contributor to their ineffectiveness in systems. So where does this dysfunctional alienation come from? Middles have their explanations: *I have little in common with the others… There are a number of them I don't particularly like… There's no potential power in this group… We bore one another… I'm not particularly interested in their areas… They are my competitors so why collaborate?… This one talks too much, that one's too emotional…* It's demons all over again.

Through the systemic lens, we see a different story. Here in our Dark Ages we are oblivious to the impact different system spaces have on us. As Tops we regularly fall into territorial struggles with one another; as Bottoms we regularly experience great pressures to conform to whatever the group opinion is; as Middles we regularly become isolated and alienated from one another.[2]

The Middle space is a diffusing space; it pulls us apart from one another and toward other individuals and groups we service or manage. We disperse. We spend our time away from one another. In that configuration our specialness becomes highlighted — our uniqueness, our separateness from one another, our differences. In the Top group we become territorial — a collection of "MINE"s; in the Bottom group we become a "WE"; and in the Middle group we become a collection of "I"s. Whatever real differences exist among us become magnified. Each of us feels unique, special, different. We feel we have little in common with one another, we feel competitive with one another, we are critical of one another, we deal at the surface with one another, we are wary of one another, and we see little potential power in us as a collectivity.

There is a vicious cycle that happens to us in the Middle space. The space pulls us apart from one another; that apartness heightens our separateness, our alienation from one another; and our alienation reinforces our staying apart — why would we want to spend time together when we have so little in common, we don't like one another, there is no potential for power in the collective, we are competitors, and so forth? So we stay apart, which reinforces the alienation, and on and on it goes. All of which is unfortunate because that Middle space is a potentially powerful space. There are productive relationships to be had and powerful contributions to be made.

---

[2] For further information on the predictable relationship problems that develop among Tops, among Middles, and among Bottoms, see B. Oshry, **Space Work**, Power & Systems, Boston, 1992.

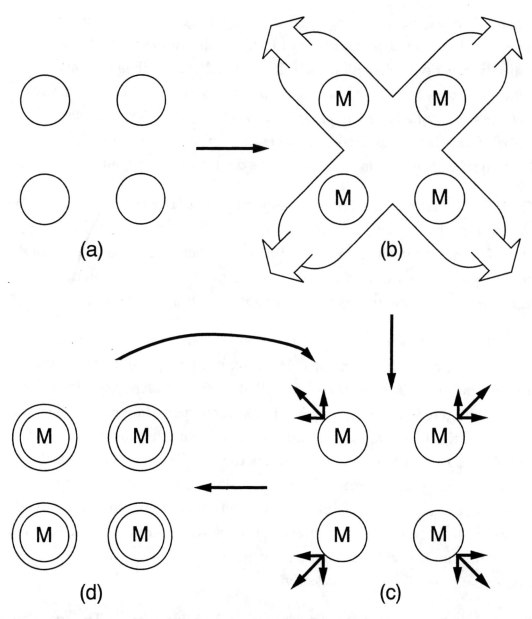

Figure 8. The vicious cycle of Middle alienation. (a) Four individuals who under other circumstances might get along perfectly well with one another... (b) enter a middle space. (c) The space pulls them apart from one another and toward the groups they service or manage. (d) In their separateness they harden into an "I-ness" mentality which reinforces their staying apart.

Middle peer groups are, potentially, the integrating mechanisms for their systems. They are in the best position to tie these systems together, to provide strong and informed leadership to their Bottoms or to the groups they service, and to create consistency, evenness and fairness throughout the system.

Middles integrate the system by integrating with one another. Each Middle moves out, manages or services his/her part of the system and collects intelligence about what is happening there; Middles come together and share their intelligence; they move back out, and then come together — moving back and forth between diffusing and integrating. Goodbye demons. Goodbye, uninformed, weak, fractionated, surpriseable, uncoordinated Middles. Through this process, the Middle space becomes the most solidly informed part of the system. Individual Middles are more knowledgeable about the total system, they are able to provide more consistent information to others, they are better able to provide guidance and direction, there is less unproductive duplication among units, there is more evenness of treatment.

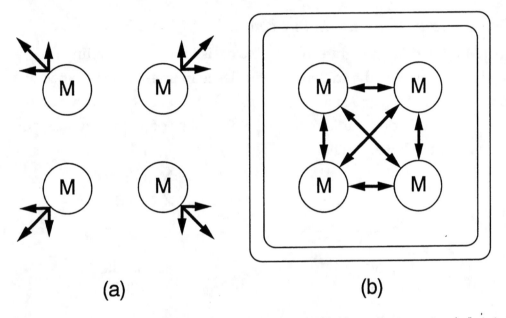

(a)   (b)

Figure 9. Middles integrate the system by integrating with one another. (a) Middles move back and forth between servicing, managing and collecting intelligence about their pieces of the system, and (b) coming together, integrating, sharing their intelligence.

Middles who integrate are a potent force in their systems. They develop a powerful support network for themselves; they provide informed leadership for others; and they lighten the burden of their Tops, making it possible for Tops to do the Top work they should be doing. This is the possibility of Middle integration. When Middles are in the grips of the middle space, however, they do not see integration as a possibility for them — "Maybe it's a good idea for some people in some circumstances but not in our organization, given the situation we're facing, and certainly not with this particular cast of characters; we have no reason to integrate, our responsibilities are diverse, we have so little in common, we don't get along, we are too competitive... " and so forth.

In the absence of a systemic lens, Middles feel that they do not integrate because of how they feel about one another. When viewed systemically, the truth is seen to be just the other way around: Middles feel the way they do as a consequence of not integrating; were they to integrate they would experience one another quite differently.

Group empowerment supports individual empowerment. Without integration Middles face the tearing pressures of the Middle space alone. With integration they create an informational and emotional base that strengthens each individual Middle.

You Don't Know What You Don't Know Until You Know It

When Middles don't integrate, there is no basis for comprehending the possibilities of empowered middleness. Middles may think that the range of possibility is from 1 to 5, and since they're at 4, that's not so bad. Only when they integrate successfully do Middles realize that the range of possibility was from 1 to 100, and 4 wasn't so hot after all.

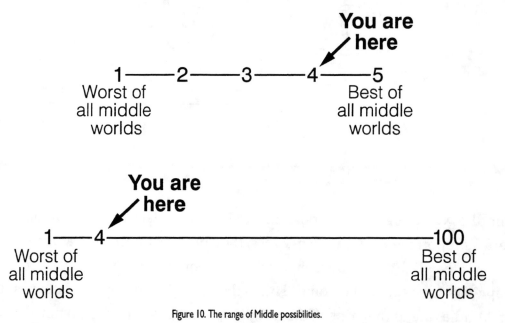

Figure 10. The range of Middle possibilities.

Middle integration creates a whole new level of possibility for Middles. From facing system pressures alone and unsupported, they become part of a powerful and supportive peer group. From being uninformed and surpriseable, they become part of the most well-informed part of the system. From being ping pong balls batted back and forth in other people's games, they become central players in creating and managing their own games.

Middles Integrating

For example, we find a Middle group in a highly sensitive chemicals plant whose members have been integrating for over seven years. According to the Plant Manager, these Middles run the day-to-day business of the plant and do it better than he ever did. These Middles like, respect and support one another — they have such a sense of teamwork that they have created their own summer and winter uniforms, they are respected by Above and Below as a strong and informed leadership team, they do their own hiring into the group, they are rewarded (50%) for how well they individually manage their units and (50%) for how well they collectively integrate the system as a whole. Their Plant Manager is liberated by this process — rather than being mired in the details of day-to-day operations, he spends his time on "Top business" — exploration of where the industry is heading and how to prepare for the future, community relations, interaction with headquarters, integration with his peers, and so forth. Not the way it usually goes with Middles.

In another setting, we find a Middle in a software company who had been having difficulty selling top management on a project idea. The Middle brought the project to the Middle group which had been integrating for several months. Without the knowledge or permission of senior management, the Middle group took on the project. All the necessary expertise was in that group — marketing, sales, production, finance and human resources. They did their research meticulously, they put together a package top management could not and did not refuse. Great pride, great teamwork, great effectiveness, and significant contribution to profitability. Not the way it usually goes with Middles.

What Are Middles Good For?

Do we really need Middles? I am asked that question regularly. The truth is: we do not need weak, uninformed, torn, confused, wishy-washy, and fractionated Middles. However, this is not the only available Middle option. Middles do have a unique perspective in organizations and special contributions to make. These can be developed only as Middles learn to see their condition systemically and learn to master the Middle space. That mastery does not come easily. To be "a Middle who stays out of the Middle" makes special demands on Middles. Middles may complain about their current "no-win" situation; yet, when they discover what it takes to empower themselves, they may decide they want no part of it.

There is great need for empowered Middles — Middles who act responsibly toward others, who are committed to their success, and who can deliver the information, direction, and support others need. The challenge for Middles is to do this while maintaining their own independence of thought and action. And that requires a different kind of fortitude, one that keeps Middles from being torn apart individually and collectively— preserving their boundaries rather than allowing them to be overrun, shaping situations rather than being shaped by them, standing up to both Above and Below, sometimes saying "no" or "not now" or "not this way" rather than dancing to every tune others play for them.

Middles who stay out of the middle, who empower themselves and others, who are Top when they can be, who are Bottom when they should be, who coach and who facilitate, and above all else, who integrate with one another — these are a different order of Middle. They value themselves and they bring value to their systems.

What Happened To The Demons?

What happened to those weak, confused, wishy-washy, fractionated, powerless Middles? They weren't sent off for therapy, they weren't replaced or fixed or fired. When Middles see and master the Middle space, the demons — like the witches of yesteryear — simply disappear.

▲▲▲▲▲▲

Acknowledgement. My thanks to Bob DuBrul for sharing with me his experiences working with middle integration.

Afterword

Still Circling

This investigation of middleness is not complete. It is as if we now stand before two doors where before there was only one. There is a beat-up, broken down old door marked "Personal". Someone keeps painting it in gaudy colors, but all the coats of paint can't hide the reality of its overuse and shabbiness. And then there is a new door marked "Systemic". Barely touched. Each door takes us to a very different set of experiences about ourselves and others, and each offers a very different set of possibilities for action, change, and system contribution. We can continue to pass through the "Personal" door or we can venture through the "Systemic" one.

You may feel that we have made great strides in unravelling the puzzle of middleness; I think we have just opened the door and are now cautiously peeking down the hall. When we really understand that this is all systemic, when we really appreciate how much we are at the mercy of systemic forces, when we really envision the possibilities that stem from mastering the Middle space, then the fun will begin.

You and I are in a Middle space. We are pulled apart from one another and toward the demands of family, work and community. And in that Middle space we experience our "I-ness," our separateness; we feel unique, that we have little in common, that there is no power in our connectedness. Consider that this is merely the illusion of the Middle space. We do have power, and that power comes from our integrating with one another.

I will continue to circle the old territory and send up reports of new discoveries. And I urge you to join the process. Test out these strategies in your life, share your experiences with me and with one another. Master the space. Integrate.

PUBLICATIONS FROM POWER & SYSTEMS, INC.
BY BARRY OSHRY

SEEING SYSTEMS: UNLOCKING THE MYSTERIES OF ORGANIZATIONAL LIFE (Berrett Koehler).

We live and work in systems, but we don't see them. System blindness costs us in terms of diminished productivity, decreased energy, and unsatisfactory relationships. *SEEING SYSTEMS* provides strategies for overcoming four types of system blindness -- spatial, temporal, relational, and process -- and opens the way to creating more powerful, productive and satisfying human systems. ISBN 1-881052-99-0. Softcover.

THE POSSIBILITIES OF ORGANIZATION

In this disarmingly simple book, Oshry strips away much of the mystery and mythology of organization life. He reveals the disempowering scenario that lies beneath all culture change efforts, strategies for developing mutual understanding and respect across organization lines, and choices that can transform your life and the life of your organization. ISBN 0-910411-10-7. Softcover.

SPACE WORK

A paradigm-shattering analysis of partnerships in the family, organization and society. Oshry reveals why potentially productive partnerships fail to develop or fall apart. And he offers systemic strategies for developing and sustaining satisfying and productive partnerships. *"Don't fix the people; help people understand and master the systemic space."* ISBN 0-910411-12-3. Softcover.

IN THE MIDDLE

Survival reading for those who know the stresses and strains of "middle" positions in organization life -- supervisors, middle managers, deans, department heads. Much needed illumination about life in the middle along with concrete strategies for converting the most overlooked and unappreciated organization position into a key contributor to total system empowerment. ISBN 0-910411-15-8. Softcover.

POWER AND POSITION

The classic text on organizational power dynamics. Appropriate for courses in Organization Behavior, Management, and Political Science. Illuminates the power dilemmas and opportunities faced by those at the top, on the bottom, and in the middle of social systems. Essential reading for serious students of power and systems. ISBN: 0-910411-04-2. Softcover.

PROGRAMS FROM
POWER & SYSTEMS, INC.

THE POWER & LEADERSHIP CONFERENCE

A six-day exploration into power and leadership for executives and managers. The PLC is a total immersion experience that focuses on people's core issues on power (discovering what it is, how you use, how you sabotage yourself), on leadership (stretching your ability), and on effecting system change (gaining a systems perspective and systems skills). You receive personal coaching that enables you to attain a higher level of effectiveness. People from all walks of life describe this as their most powerful and productive learning experience ever.

THE ORGANIZATION WORKSHOP: CREATING PARTNERSHIP

A two day public workshop and in-house workshop for your work team, department or division. The Organization Workshop helps build the human systems needed to deal with the critical business issues your organization faces. The workshop illuminates the pitfalls and the possibilities of developing partnership among top executives, middle managers, workers and customers. Focuses on strategies for building and sustaining partnership throughout the organization and with the customer. It lays the foundation for developing a workforce that is flexible, can adapt readily to rapidly changing conditions, and where people work in partnership up, down and across organization lines. A training and licensing program is available for this workshop.

CREATING COMMUNITY IN THE FACE OF DIFFERENCE

Dominance lies at the heart of many of our most critical organizational and societal issues. This workshop highlights the systemic role of dominance in creating community in the organization and in society. The session addresses the challenge of building robust communities when there is a dominant culture and "other" cultures who all need to work and live together.

PLEASE CONTACT US FOR DETAILED INFORMATION ON OUR PUBLICATIONS AND PROGRAMS.

Power & Systems, Inc.
P.O. Box 990288
Prudential Station
Boston, MA 02199-0288

tel. 1.800.241.0598 or 617.437.1640
fax 1.617.437.6713

ABOUT BARRY OSHRY

Barry Oshry is the Founder of Power & Systems, Inc. of Boston. Power & Systems' network of Training Associates teaches the principles of total system empowerment to organizations and institutions throughout the world.

Prior to founding Power & Systems in 1975, Barry Oshry served as Chairman of the Organization Behavior Department at Boston University. He is a pioneer in the study of power and empowerment and in the development of educational programs addressing these and other social system issues.

Power & Systems' high-impact educational programs have been hailed as major breakthroughs in illuminating the possibilities and challenges of organizational and community life.

In addition to his research, writing and teaching, Barry Oshry has been poet, playwright, bartender, department store manager, waiter, and greeting card designer. He lives in Boston with his partner and wife, Karen Ellis Oshry.

PUBLICATION ORDER FORM

TITLE	NO.	COST	TOTAL
SEEING SYSTEMS	____	$22.95	_____
THE POSSIBILITIES OF ORGANIZATION	____	$19.95	_____
SPACE WORK	____	$13.95	_____
IN THE MIDDLE	____	$18.95	_____
POWER AND POSITION	____	$13.95	_____
MASS. ORDERS ADD 5% SALES TAX:			_____
SHIPPING:			_____
TOTAL:			_____

QUANTITY DISCOUNTS:
10-49 COPIES/TITLE: LESS 10%
50 OR MORE COPIES/TITLE: LESS 15%

U.S. SHIPPING
$4.50 FOR THE FIRST BOOK. ADD $1.50 FOR EACH ADDITIONAL BOOK. ORDERS ARE SHIPPED UPS. ORDERS UNDER $50 MUST BE PREPAID BY CHECK, MONEY ORDER, VISA, MASTERCARD OR AMERICAN EXPRESS.

❑ CREDIT CARD: ___AMEX ___MC ___VISA
   CARD NO: _____
   EXPIRATION DATE: _____ SIGNATURE _____

❑ MY CHECK IS ENCLOSED (PAYABLE TO POWER & SYSTEMS, INC.)

❑ PURCHASE ORDER #_____

NAME_____
COMPANY_____
ADDRESS_____
CITY_____STATE_____ZIP_____
TEL. NO._____

MAIL TO: POWER & SYSTEMS, INC.   **FAX:** 617.437.6713
P.O. BOX 990288
PRUDENTIAL STATION   **TEL:** 1.800.241.0598 OR
BOSTON, MA 02199-0288   617.437.1640